Sweet Cane

Sweet Cane

The Architecture of the Sugar Works of East Florida

Lucy B. Wayne

THE UNIVERSITY OF ALABAMA PRESS
Tuscaloosa

Typeface: ACaslon

∞

The paper on which this book is printed meets the minimum requirements of American
National Standard for Information Sciences-Permanence of Paper for Printed Library
Materials, ANSI Z39.48-1984.

Library of Congress Cataloging-in-Publication Data

Wayne, Lucy B. (Lucy Bowles), 1947–
    Sweet cane : the architecture of the sugar works of East Florida / Lucy B. Wayne.
       p.   cm.
    Includes bibliographical references and index.
MISBN 978-0-8173-1696-9 (cloth : alk. paper) — ISBN 978-0-8173-5592-0 (paper : alk.
paper) — ISBN 978-0-8173-8287-2 (electronic) 1. Sugar plantations—East Florida—History.
2. Sugarcane industry—East Florida—History. 3. Mills and mill-work—East Florida—History.
4. Architecture, Industrial—East Florida—History. 5. Masonry—East Florida—History.
6. Historic buildings—East Florida. 7. Historic sites—East Florida. 8. Industrial archaeology—
East Florida. 9. East Florida—History, Local. 10. East Florida—Antiquities. I. Title.
    F312.W39   2010
    975.9′18—dc22

                                                                           2009047699

Cover. *The Ruins of the Sugar House,* by John Rogers Vinton, 1843. (Courtesy of the Sam and
Robbie Vickers Florida Collection)

To my parents, John and Jane Bowles,
for instilling a love of learning and of history in me.

To Alex and Michelle for all the joy.

Most of all to Marty for providing
unconditional support and love.

Contents

List of Illustrations   ix

Acknowledgments   xiii

PART I. SUGAR AND PLANTATIONS   1

1. Introduction   3

2. Plantations as Industrial Complexes   10

3. Sweet Cane   14

4. Sugar in East Florida   35

PART II. THE ARCHITECTURE OF EAST FLORIDA
SUGAR PLANTATIONS   45

5. Architectural Influences   47

6. The Spanish Trains: Oswald/Yonge Three Chimneys and McHardy   52

7. The Adaptive Sugar Works: Dummett and Spring Garden   73

8. The Fully Evolved Sugar Works: Bulow, Macrae, Cruger-DePeyster,
    and Dunlawton   98

9. The End of an Industry   148

References Cited   155

Index   169

Illustrations

Figures

1. Location of East Florida sugar works   4
2. Sugar cane (*Saccharum officinarum L.*)   15
3. Planting sugar cane in Antigua, West Indies   18
4. Harvesting sugar cane in Antigua, West Indies   20
5. Seventeenth-century sugar works in the Antilles   21
6. Idealized ground plan for sugar works   22
7. Animal-powered vertical sugar mill   23
8. Williams animal-powered horizontal sugar mill   24
9. Steam-powered horizontal sugar cane mill and cane carrier   24
10. Spanish sugar train   27
11. Jamaica sugar train   27
12. Boiling sugar and sugar cones   29
13. Sugar boiling house in Antigua, West Indies   30
14. Sugar purgery or curing house   32
15. Rum distillery   34
16. Fagan House at Oswald/Yonge Three Chimneys   57
17. South side of Oswald/Yonge Three Chimneys sugar train   58
18. Plan of Oswald/Yonge Three Chimneys sugar works   59
19. Looking east at Oswald/Yonge Three Chimneys sugar train   60
20. North side of Oswald/Yonge Three Chimneys sugar train   61
21. Flue under *grande* kettle, Oswald/Yonge Three Chimneys   62

22. Looking west at Oswald/Yonge Three Chimneys sugar train   62

23. North side of distillery, Oswald/Yonge sugar works   64

24. South side of distillery, Oswald/Yonge sugar works   64

25. Distillery at Three Chimneys, ca. 1910   65

26. Southeast side of McHardy sugar train and well   69

27. Plan of McHardy sugar works   70

28. Detail of McHardy sugar train chimney   71

29. Berry's Premium Firebrick, McHardy sugar works   71

30. Sugar works in Surinam   75

31. Semi-portable steam engine   78

32. Looking northeast at Dummett sugar works   80

33. Looking southwest at Dummett sugar works   81

34. Plan of Dummett sugar works   82

35. Interior of Dummett sugar works, ca. 1935   83

36. Exterior of Dummett sugar works, ca. 1935   84

37. Elevation of Dummett sugar works   84

38. Engine firebox at Dummett sugar works   85

39. Wall arch at Dummett sugar works   86

40. Looking northeast at Rees Spring Garden sugar works   89

41. Spring Garden waterwheel in late nineteenth century   94

42. Spring Garden modern waterwheel   94

43. Plan of Spring Garden sugar works   95

44. South side of Spring Garden sugar train   95

45. Spring Garden, ca. 1912   96

46. Looking west at Bulow sugar works   103

47. Plan of Bulow sugar works   104

48. Looking north at Bulow engine house   105

49. Northeast corner of Bulow engine house   106

50. Looking southeast at Bulow boiling house   107

51. South facade, Bulow storage/loading room   108

52. East purgery of Bulow sugar works   109

53. Bulow spring house   110

54. Looking southwest at Macrae sugar works   113

55. Plan of Macrae sugar works   114

56. Macrae engine/boiler/crusher area   115

57. Looking southeast at Macrae sugar train   116

58. Firebox of Macrae sugar train   116

59. Macrae sugar works octagonal well   117

60. Looking east at purgery and cistern of Macrae sugar works   118

61. *The Ruins of the Sugar House,* by John Rogers Vinton, 1843 (courtesy of the Sam and Robbie Vickers Florida Collection)   121

62. Looking north at Cruger-DePeyster sugar works   123

63. Plan of Cruger-DePeyster sugar works   124

64. Looking east at Cruger-DePeyster engine house   125

65. Looking southwest at Cruger-DePeyster engine house and well   126

66. Looking northeast at Cruger-DePeyster boiling room   127

67. Looking southwest at chimney area of Cruger-DePeyster   128

68. Looking southwest at purgery of Cruger-DePeyster   129

69. Plan of Dunlawton sugar works   135

70. Looking northeast at Dunlawton sugar works   136

71. Dunlawton sugar works, 1875   136

72. Northeast exterior wall at Dunlawton sugar works   137

73. Engine and boiler at Dunlawton sugar works   138

74. Engine house flue at Dunlawton sugar works   139

75. Firebox engine house chimney at Dunlawton sugar works   140

76. Wagon stops at cane crusher at Dunlawton sugar works   140

77. Cane crusher at Dunlawton sugar works   141

78. Looking north at boiling house of Dunlawton sugar works   143

79. South train flue controls at Dunlawton sugar works   144

80. South train firebox at Dunlawton sugar works   145

81. Looking northwest at purgery of Dunlawton sugar works   146

82. Comparison of East Florida sugar works plans   149

Table

1. List of East Florida sugar plantation sites   8

Acknowledgments

Over the past 15 years a number of archaeological and architectural studies have been completed at the sites described in this book, but the information obtained from these studies is primarily confined to the world of "gray," or unpublished, literature. This book is based on that body of work and its many dedicated researchers. Major contributions came from the historic research of Dr. Patricia C. Griffin at all of the sites, but especially at Spring Garden; the architectural work of Herschel E. Shepard Jr., FAIA, and Gregory Hall, AIA, at all of the sites; archaeological research by Ted Payne at all of the sites, but particularly at Three Chimneys and Spring Garden; and the work of the author's company, SouthArc, at all of the sites.

But this study would not exist without the many research projects that have been completed at all of these sites. In addition to the colleagues cited above, I would like to acknowledge the work of these scholars and writers: journalist Charles Coe at Cruger-DePeyster; archaeologist John Griffin at Cruger-DePeyster, McHardy, Dummett, and Bulow; engineer Greville Bathe at Dunlawton; architect I. S. K. Reeves V and archaeologist Marilyn Stewart at Dunlawton; archaeologist Bruce Piatek at Dunlawton and Cruger-DePeyster; an archaeological team from the Florida Bureau of Historic Sites and Properties, led by Randy Daniel, at Bulow and McHardy; archaeologists Robin Denson and Gary Ellis of GARI at Spring Garden; and Marsha Chance, Greg Smith, and Keith Ashley of Environmental Services, Inc., at Cruger-DePeyster. This book draws heavily from the work completed at these sites, and the author commends these scholars for their careful research and documentation.

I owe a debt to many people for assistance in this work. Dr. Jay Bushnell, former president of the Volusia Anthropological Society, Tom Scofield, formerly of Volusia County Planning, and Benny Woodham of Tomoka Basin GeoPark, were instrumental in obtaining a state grant which permitted the documentation and development of preservation and interpretation plans for the eight East Florida sugar works included in this volume. The work completed for that project provided the idea for this book. The Volusia Anthropological Society, Ormond Beach Historical Trust, Volusia County, and Tomoka Basin GeoPark all contributed time and funds to assist that grant project. Research at Spring Garden and Dunlawton was also completed under state grants. The Florida Division of Historical Resources is to be commended for their support of these and other historic preservation projects. Additional work at Dunlawton and Cruger-DePeyster was conducted with the support of Volusia County.

Many individuals contributed their knowledge and expertise throughout the sugar works grant project; this assistance is reflected in the contents of this book. These people include: Walt Marder of the Florida Division of Historical Resources; historian Daniel Schafer of the University of North Florida; local historians Alice Strickland and Harold Cardwell; Tom Scofield, formerly of Volusia County Planning; Benny Woodham of Tomoka Basin GeoPark; James Cusick of the P. K. Yonge Library of Florida History at the University of Florida; and Shirley Warner, Justin Warner, and Ceylon Barclay of the Ormond Beach Historical Trust.

In terms of this book, the late Dr. Thomas Eubanks's research at McIntosh plantation in southeastern Georgia and on Tobago in the West Indies provided an invaluable study of the history of sugar, its growth, and production. Chuck Meide of the St. Augustine Lighthouse generously shared his work on Caribbean sugar works. Ted Payne has been generous with the information he obtained from his studies at Dummett, Three Chimneys, and DeLeon Springs.

Tom Baskett of Volusia County provided information on interpretation that is being completed for several of the sites and, more importantly, paved the way for obtaining the use of the Vickers Collection painting on the cover of this book. Sam Vickers, owner of this painting, graciously gave permission for its use. Fayn LeVeille of the Halifax Historical Society, Adam Watson of the Florida State Archives Florida Memory Project collection, and Susan Danforth of the John Carter Brown Library provided assistance and copies for illustrations used in this book.

Dr. Jerald Milanich, American Institute of Archaeology editor, well-published author, and widely known Florida archaeologist, provided advice and guidance in the revision of the initial manuscript. The three press-selected reviewers of the initial two versions of this manuscript pointed out weaknesses and inspired me to rethink some sections of the manuscript.

I owe a special debt of gratitude to Dr. Patricia Griffin, who has conducted the most important historic research on these sites in recent years. Pat has been endlessly willing to share her knowledge and has been very kind and supportive to me in this endeavor—including answering endless questions about the publishing process. She was also willing to read and comment on the first draft of this manuscript.

Herschel E. Shepard Jr., FAIA, was an early proponent of preservation of the sugar works and is familiar with all of the properties. Herschel introduced me to my first sugar plantation, Dunlawton in Port Orange, Florida, and has provided encouragement, advice, and information since that time. His expertise in the preservation of historic structures has been invaluable throughout the study of these sites. Most importantly, he was willing to read and comment on the draft of this book. Herschel has been both teacher and colleague; his input is always appreciated. I am tremendously honored that he has taken an interest in this project.

The staff of SouthArc, Inc., has been supportive, encouraging, and helpful throughout this process. Kelly Christiansen, Anne Coleman, and Andy Belcourt read versions of the final manuscript and caught many errors. I would especially like to thank John Davidson, who created the original graphics for the book and was cheerful and endlessly patient with my changes and additions. John also helped find and select the original photographs taken by SouthArc during earlier sugar works projects. My business partner, Martin Dickinson, provided support, encouragement, and assistance with graphics and photography, along with productive criticism of this work. Many thanks to Linnea Dwyer of Linnaeus Indexing Service for completing the challenging task of indexing, which was well beyond my capabilities.

A big thanks, also, goes to Judith Knight of the University of Alabama Press, who was willing to take a chance on this study and guide me through the revision and publication process. Copy editor Lady Vowell Smith painstakingly reviewed the manuscript and caught my many, many errors. Any remaining errors or omissions are solely my responsibility.

And last, but certainly not least, I wish to thank my family for their continued support of my enthusiasm for old ruins.

Lucy B. Wayne

I
Sugar and Plantations

Sugar cane will prosper and perhaps do well, but the labor necessary to produce a good crop is great, great, great.

> —John James Audubon, letter to editor of
> the *American Monthly Journal of Geology*,
> December 31, 1831 (qtd. in Alice Strickland,
> *Ashes on the Wind*)

1
Introduction

[A] source of wealth opened.
—Charles Vignoles, *Observations upon the Floridas* (1823)

Today the remains of the late-eighteenth- to early-nineteenth-century sugar plantations of East Florida lie in the parks and forests of the region (Figure 1). Although a few are accessible to the public with interpretative exhibits, others lie hidden, slowly disintegrating and almost forgotten. This study is intended to help explain the plantation ruins in order to provide a better understanding of their history and architecture.

Sugar Production in Florida

Sugar has been a Florida agricultural product on at least a limited basis since the early years of the first European settlements. From the late eighteenth century to 1835, the heart of the sugar industry was concentrated in what was known as East Florida, particularly today's Volusia County.

By the 1830s, at least 22 plantations, described as "the most valuable plantations in Florida" (Mahon 1985:102), were in operation in this region, "so that the economic development of this short stretch of the upper east coast exceeded that of any other part of the territory" (Boyd 1951:59). But, by the end of January 1836, "the whole industry was destroyed" during the initial attacks of the Second Seminole War (Mahon 1985:102). Sugar and the sugar works that produced it would never regain their importance in East Florida. Only two of the sugar works would even be rebuilt.

In the period between the end of the Second Seminole War in 1842 and the Civil War in 1861, a second group of sugar plantations was built in Central Florida and along the lower Florida Gulf Coast. But competition from the massive sugar plantations of Louisiana and the Caribbean limited the success of this particular crop in Florida in those years leading up to the Civil War. The war itself, combined with emancipation of the slaves vital to sugar growth and production, effectively ended the sugar industry in Florida until the late nineteenth century brought sugar

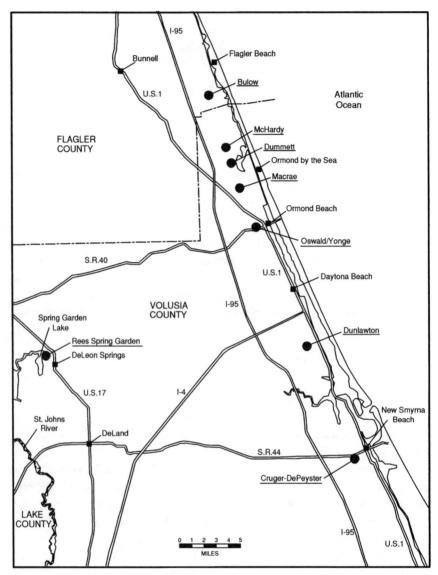

1. Location of East Florida sugar works.

to the Everglades, along with modern processing factories. Today sugar production remains a major agricultural industry in South Florida.

The East Florida Sugar Plantations

The history and architecture of the East Florida plantations are little known outside the immediate area. I had lived in Florida for 15 years and had been a professional archaeologist for 10 years before I realized that these sites even existed or learned their history. In 1991, I was introduced to this industry at Dunlawton sugar works in Port Orange (Wayne et al. 1991). Several years later I was involved in a project at Oswald's Three Chimneys site (Wayne et al. 1999) which gave me insight on the earliest period of sugar in Florida. Two years after that, I helped develop structural evaluations and stabilization plans for eight of the East Florida sugar works, including Dunlawton and Three Chimneys (Wayne et al. 2001). That exposure to the variety and range of sites in this relatively compact geographic area formed the idea for this study.

It was clear to me that the sites themselves present a fascinating remnant of what was once an important regional industry, as well as examples of masonry construction and early industrial engineering. This study is an effort to open the door on these fascinating ruins and tell their stories as reflected in their architecture. It is above all an architectural history. It is not a regional history or a socioeconomic history, nor is it an attempt to look at the New World sugar industry as a whole.

Although these sugar works were part of plantations, I am not looking at the plantations as a whole, or the houses of the owners and the slave labor force—primarily because we have very little information about the other components of most of these sites. It is the masonry sugar works that have lasted and are visible today.

My goal is to provide sufficient information on the sugar industry and the historic events that affected that industry in East Florida so that those interested in these structures will better understand what they see and what the structures represent. As architectural historian Camille Wells says: "[H]istoric architecture is one aspect of the past that we can still see, touch, experience . . . and part of what attracts us to old buildings is their insistence on communicating, in some outmoded dialect we do not entirely understand, the energy and purpose, the achievements and hopes, the disappointments and hardships of those who made and used them" (Wells 1995:3).

The Setting

All of the sugar works discussed in this book are now in public ownership, although two are not currently accessible to the general public. All eight sites are in what was once known as East Florida, with seven in Volusia County and one in adjacent southern Flagler County (Figure 1). Historically, East Florida was defined during the British Period (1763 to 1783) as the area east of the Apalachicola River in the Florida Panhandle, extending north to the St. Marys River and east to the Atlantic Ocean (Gordon 2002:164). In reality, there was little settlement in the central area between the Apalachicola River and the St. Johns River until after the Second Seminole War ended in 1842. Between the initial colonization of Florida in the First Spanish Period until after 1842, the majority of the settlement of East Florida was between the St. Johns River on the west, the Atlantic Ocean on the east, Cape Canaveral on the south, and the northern border of the territory on the St. Marys River. Volusia and Flagler counties lie squarely within this region, with both counties extending from the St. Johns River to the Atlantic Ocean.

All of the sites share certain geographic characteristics. Each property has access to water transportation (Griffin 1999:5), a vital resource in a land without railroads and with an extremely poor road system. Seven of the sites are on the estuarine rivers draining into the Atlantic Ocean in what is known as the Halifax region, while the eighth (Spring Garden) is on the St. Johns River, which ultimately flows into the Atlantic. With the exception of Spring Garden, the sites were also located along the King's Road, one of Florida's original roads that ran from south of New Smyrna Beach north to the St. Marys River, connecting the coastal areas of Florida and Georgia. While the King's Road would not have provided the dependable and fast transportation offered by water, it did provide an alternative, as well as access between neighboring plantations.

Climate was another important factor shared by these properties (Griffin 1999:6). In all cases, the plantations are buffered from storms by either the barrier islands or an inland location. Florida is blessed with a humid, temperate climate that alternates between a cool dry season and a warm wet season. This variation, along with normally abundant yearly rainfall, supports lush vegetation growth. Damaging frosts are infrequent, particularly in the coastal region, due to the moderating effect of the ocean. This allows for a lengthy growing season and, in some cases, multiple harvests (Chen and Gerber 1990:11–12). As topographical engineer Charles Vignoles said of Florida in 1823: "the great length of summer, or period of absolute elevation of the thermometer above the freezing point, allows the cane to ripen much higher than that in Louisiana" (Vignoles 1823:96–97).

Soils are another factor in the successful development of these properties. Florida's upland soils are primarily sands with relatively low levels of nutrients (Myers and Ewel 1990:3). However, in moderately to poorly drained areas, the damp soils become mixed with organic materials which provide the nutrients otherwise lacking. In addition, these sand-humus mixtures are easy to cultivate (Griffin 1999:5). Vignoles claimed that "the recent successful trials that have been made upon it [sugar], have determined the curious fact that it will grow in almost any of the soils of Florida, south of the mouth of the St. Johns river" (Vignoles 1823:96–97).

A final factor that may have influenced development of the plantations in this region is the relative lack of settlement prior to the British Period of 1763 to 1783. In the period preceding modern agricultural methods and fertilizers, the tendency of planters to repeatedly plant the same cash crops depleted soil fertility. The previous lack of settlement meant that these areas had not been cultivated, and thus retained whatever natural fertility was available.

Organization of the Study

In writing this book, I have attempted to correlate the historic, archaeological, and architectural information that is available on the eight sites that form the focus of the study. Based on my own experience at these sites, I believe that the variations in the architecture of these structures reflect five factors: (1) technological advances in sugar production, (2) the influence of the Caribbean and Georgia sugar plantations, (3) the increased value of sugar as a product in this region, (4) the incorporation of formal architectural details into what was essentially industrial buildings, and (5) adaptations to the local environment and resources.

During the period in which these plantations flourished, there was a shift from a very basic level of sugar production based on human or animal power, to more sophisticated operations using water, wind (in the Caribbean), and steam. As the sophistication of the means of production increased, the size and complexity of the sugar works themselves developed. The increase in size also reflects the growing value of the products—sugar, molasses, and sometimes rum. The greater wealth of the planters—or simply the larger investment—led them to use more expensive, permanent materials (brick and stone), as well as stylistic touches such as quoin blocks on the corners and scored stucco coatings, which graphically displayed their vision of success, wealth, and power. And one cannot discount the influence of the older Caribbean and Georgian sugar works.

Finally, all structures reflect adaptation to their environment to some extent. These adaptations at the sugar works range from the specific source of power used (animal, water, steam) to the materials of which they are constructed—in this case, often the local stone known as coquina.

In order to understand these various architectural changes and influences, it is necessary to understand the history of the sites, the nature of sugar cultivation and production, and the changes that occurred in that production through time. It is also necessary to place these sites in the context of the local plantation economy.

Part 1 of this study will discuss the nature of sugar plantations as industrial sites, and describe sugar growth and the production of sugar, molasses, and rum. It will also discuss the development of this plantation industry in East Florida and its subsequent demise. Part 2 will highlight the eight specific plantations and sugar works remains, which reflect the early, adaptive, and fully evolved forms of the sugar works.

All of the sites in this book are eligible for the National Register of Historic Places in multiple categories: history, technology, architecture, and archaeology. Three are listed on the Register at the present time, and one has been submitted for listing. Table 1 provides a list of the sites with their location, ownership, and National Register status.

Two of the sites, Oswald-Yonge's Three Chimneys and the sugar train of the

Table 1. List of East Florida Sugar Plantation Sites

Site No.	Name	Location	Ownership	NRHP Status*
8Vo196	Oswald/Yonge (Swamp Settlement/ Three Chimneys)	Ormond Beach, Volusia County	State	Eligible
8Vo244	McHardy	Tomoka Basin GeoPark, Volusia County	State	Eligible
8Vo241	Dummett Grove	Tomoka Basin GeoPark, Volusia County	State	Eligible
8Vo30	Rees Spring Garden	DeLeon Springs State Park Volusia County	State	Eligible
8FL7	Bulow	Bulow Plantation Ruins State Historic Park, Flagler County	State	Listed
8Vo193	Macrae	Tomoka Basin GeoPark, Volusia County	State	Eligible
8Vo184	Cruger-DePeyster	New Smyrna Sugar Mill Ruins State Historic Site, Volusia County	State	Listed
8Vo189	Dunlawton	Sugar Mill Botanical Gardens Port Orange, Volusia County	County	Listed

*Listing on National Register of Historic Places

McHardy property, reflect the earliest simple form of sugar works, prior to the introduction of steam or water power. One of Dunlawton's two sugar trains may also have its origin in this period. Dummett, the final form of McHardy and Rees Spring Garden is from the middle, adaptive period, when new systems were introduced and the structures became more substantial. The remaining sites, Bulow, Addison-Macrae, Cruger-DePeyster, and the final form of Dunlawton, represent the full development of the process, as well as the use of stylistic architectural features—particularly masonry details. These fully developed sugar works are also the most closely related to their Caribbean predecessors and similar sites in southeastern Georgia.

Interestingly, but perhaps not surprisingly, a number of the properties in this study were developed by people related through blood or marriage to the owners of similar properties; it was, after all, a small population and very much a frontier throughout the sugar period. In all cases, a strong Caribbean connection was present, not only due to the shared products and processing system, but also from engineers, operators, and builders with Caribbean roots. Planter Thomas Spalding of southeast Georgia also claimed that it was through sugar production in Georgia that the Florida plantations got their start (Floyd 1937:92). Given the proximity of the two areas, as well as familial ties in some cases, it is likely that the Georgia sugar works did influence the final forms in East Florida.

2
Plantations as Industrial Complexes

> It makes good sense to view the plantations as a synthesis of field and
> factory.
>
> —Sidney W. Mintz, *Sweetness and Power:*
> *The Place of Sugar in Modern History* (1985)

Since the sites in this book are parts of plantations, it is appropriate to examine
how a plantation differs from a farm. Traditionally, the southern plantation system
has been viewed as an outgrowth of the mercantilism of the eighteenth and early
nineteenth centuries, in which the industrialized world markets such as England
and the northern United States demanded raw materials. In exchange for these
raw materials, the plantations were supplied with manufactured products (Zierdan
1986:33). Sugar and its by-products, molasses and rum, were integral products in
this system and were particularly tied to the infamous triangular slave trade between New England, Africa, and the sugar plantations of the Caribbean—and, for
a short period, Florida. In this triangle, sugar, and particularly molasses, were sent
north via the same New England shipping companies that sailed to Africa to acquire slaves who were then sold to the sugar planters.

Defining a Plantation

In 1955, geographer Merle Prunty identified six distinguishing characteristics of
the plantation system: (1) a landholding larger than a family farm; (2) division of
management (the owner) and labor; (3) specialized crop production; (4) location in
a region with a plantation tradition; (5) spatial organization that reflected centralized control of the cultivation power; and (6) a relatively large input of cultivation
power per acre (Prunty 1955:460). A "plantation" is not defined solely by the labor
system, as that is only one element of the whole. According to Prunty, all six elements are necessary to characterize a holding as a plantation (Prunty 1955:460). It
should be noted that Prunty did not emphasize production of a staple crop; rather,
the important criterion was production of a specialized crop or crops destined for
cash sale (Orser 1984:1). The human labor involved could be slaves, indentured servants, free labor, or some combination of the three. In return for their efforts, the

labor may have been provided with wages, a portion of the crop, housing, food, clothing, or other goods and services (Adams 1987:9).

The southern plantation system can also be characterized as a system with wide variations in size, products, labor systems, location, degree of diversification, and markets. However, certain factors remained consistent. First, the plantation was always, in a sense, a frontier institution, functioning as a relatively self-sufficient system on the periphery of the world market. Second, there was almost always an identifiable element of status differentiation, both within individual plantations and between plantations in the same region. Third, the settlement pattern reflected centralized control over the means of production, whether this was the workers themselves in the antebellum plantations, or the tools, animals, machines, and seeds in the later tenant farm system. At the individual plantation level, this settlement pattern was also affected by seasonality of production, nature of resource processing, environmental requirements of the specific products, transportation methods, storage requirements, defense needs, and any specialized functions within the system (Adams 1987:9–10).

Archaeologist Theresa Singleton has pointed out that "A plantation system embraces all the connecting and supporting institutions associated with the plantation settlement. Only within this purview is it possible to understand any one aspect of plantation history, culture, or society" (Singleton 1985:2). All of the plantations discussed in this study included dwellings for the owners, overseers, and slaves; associated outbuildings and agricultural structures; roads; and other land modifications such as ditches and landings. They also usually produced multiple crops, some of which were equally important as market products (i.e., rice, indigo, and cotton). While Singleton is correct in her statement that in order to fully understand a plantation one must look at the entire system, as well as its interrelationship with the region and the world market, the scope of this study will be limited to the industrial aspect of these plantations—the sugar works. Thus the emphasis will be on the process and the architecture, rather than the plantations as a whole.

In reality, we know very little about the owners' complexes and slave cabins at the eight sites in this study. Owners' houses have been definitely identified or described at only two of the properties, Bulow and Dummett. Two others (McHardy and Macrae) have house remains that may be associated with their respective sugar works, but the records are not entirely clear. One other site (Oswald/Yonge Three Chimneys) has a limited description of houses, but the locations are not known. In all cases where we have any information, the houses were modest affairs, completely unlike the Great Houses of Caribbean sugar plantations or the mansions of many Louisiana sugar plantations. Even less information is available on slave components. The location of the slave cabins is positively known for only two of the sites, Bulow and Dummett, and very little archaeological research has been conducted at either location. Although the information we have on these components will be briefly addressed in the historic discussion of each site, the focus remains on the visible remains—the sugar works themselves.

Plantations as Industries

Social historian Eugene Genovese (1962:422–423) states that the willingness of the South to embrace the plantation system led directly to a lack of industrial development within that region. From the perspective of having factories full of machinery, Genovese is correct. However, sugar cane, like other major plantation crops—rice, cotton, and indigo—requires processing prior to shipment. In fact, the production of sugar, molasses, and rum is essentially a manufacturing process, and the sugar makers were among the early users of steam-powered equipment. Construction of the sugar works themselves required a degree of engineering expertise, while the manufacturing process was conducted under the direction of a skilled sugar maker. Operation and maintenance of the steam system and the equipment it powered also required expertise.

Archaeologist William Adams has pointed out that plantations are essentially agricultural factories in which capital investment is represented by acquisition of land and buildings, the means of production is the reliable labor source (slavery in this case), and an agricultural product is sold on the market (Adams 1987:9).

Historian Sidney Mintz (1985:51–52) argues that there are several factors in particular that make the sugar plantation an agro-industry: (1) the combination of agricultural production and raw material processing under one authority; (2) division of the labor force into skilled and unskilled workers organized to meet the overall production goals; (3) a "time-conscious" system due to the processing needs of the ripe cane itself, which required strict scheduling; (4) "the separation of production from consumption"; and (5) "the separation of the worker from his tools."

As sugar and rum production increased in value, there were corresponding developments in the way the raw materials were processed and the end products generated. These changes are partly a result of the need for greater production, but also of technological developments in the early nineteenth century. Production changes are reflected in the architecture of the sugar works themselves, primarily in their greater complexity, an increase in their size, and the introduction of steam power. At the same time, as previously indicated, the wealth expected and afforded by the cash products is reflected in the architecture. This included more substantial masonry construction, as well as stylistic touches to indicate the sophistication and wealth of the owner, and the substantial financial investment. By the end of the sugar boom period in East Florida, the sugar works were showplaces of the plantations, consisting of large masonry buildings with symmetrical layouts and sometimes arched openings.

Sugar Labor

Sugar production in East Florida relied on slave labor. While historian Larry Rivers (2000:18) says that sugar cultivation was "an effort often associated with the harshest slave-labor conditions," in reality it was probably no worse than the cultivation systems of indigo or rice, both crops grown in East Florida. One writer has pointed out that "Sugar production, because of the necessity of promptly refining the newly harvested crop, included industrial processes unique in southern agriculture and employed a disproportionate number of males" (Faust 1991:13).

In describing sugar plantation slavery in the Caribbean, one historian has estimated that the minimum size for profitable production was 300 acres and 30 slaves. This would result in a yield of about 50 hogsheads of sugar. Doubling the slave force and livestock would produce twice as much sugar with no increase in acreage. Creating unduly large plantations was not worth it, since the size that yielded maximum profit was tied to how much cane could be transported from field to mill and milled within 24 hours of cutting (Halcrow 1982:67). As another writer points out, "bottlenecks in production remained principally in rates of harvest" (Meniketti 2006:63).

Varying estimates of the number of laborers and their skills can be found in the literature on sugar. A 1789 description of a Jamaican sugar plantation states that there were 60 cane cutters and 38 factory workers. The factory workers consisted of a mix of half skilled and half semi-skilled workers. The skilled workers were identified as 10 boilers, 5 distillers, 3 potters, and 1 cooper (Halcrow 1982:79). Writing in the early nineteenth century, sugar planter Thomas Spalding of Georgia identified 62 slaves for a 100-acre plantation as follows: 9 in the boiling house, 7 in the mill house, 13 minding livestock and driving carts, and 33 cutting and loading cane in the fields. He also noted that 20 horses, mules, and oxen were needed for milling, and 4 oxcarts with 12 oxen were needed to bring the cane from the fields (Spalding 1816:248). In addition to the slaves, the planter would need overseers and an experienced sugar maker. If using steam, he would also need a mechanic familiar with the engine in order to keep it operating.

Overall, sugar production for market was not a poor man's or small planter's crop of choice. As J. Brummell, a mid-nineteenth-century visitor to Jamaica, stated, "The plain truth is, a poor man has no business with a sugar estate" (qtd. in Halcrow 1982:66). A successful sugar planter either had money or had the collateral necessary to borrow it (Halcrow 1982:66).

3
Sweet Cane

We will now proceed to consider in our arrangement the best and only
approved method of cultivating the Cane, with a description of the most
economical buildings for the manufacture of Sugar.
          —John C. Cleland, *The Superior Advantages to Be Derived
          from the Culture of Sugar-Cane, in East-Florida* (1836)

If we are going to look at plantations that were involved in producing one of
Florida's first commercial products, sugar, it is useful to have an understanding
of how the sugar and rum-making processes work in order to understand the remains of the factories themselves. Although sugar, or sucrose, naturally occurs
in plants, and a wide variety of fruit juices and syrups can be used as sweeteners,
the grass known as sugar cane, *Saccharum* sp., is the plant of interest in this study
(Figure 2). Its use was first recorded in India over 2,000 years ago. By A.D. 1000
several varieties of cane were used, including the wild *Saccharum spontaneum* and
the domesticated *Saccharum officinarum* and *Saccharum barberi Jeswiet*. Although
used as a sweetener in India, its primary early usage was as a medicine (Galloway
1989:19–21).

A Brief History of Sugar

By the tenth century, sugar cane had spread from India to the Middle East. The
Crusaders would introduce it to Europe, where it was initially limited to use as a
medicine, and as a food and drink additive for the very wealthy. Growth and production gradually spread around the Mediterranean, at first to Spain and then to
Sicily, Crete, and Cyprus. Less successful attempts were made in Rhodes, Malta,
southern Italy and Greece, Portugal, Tuscany, Provence, and Turkey (Galloway
1989:24–34).

Between 1450 and 1680, Spain and Portugal monopolized sugar production for
the European market (Galloway 1989:48). The raw sugar was shipped to Venice,
Bologna, or Antwerp, where it was further refined (Galloway 1989:40). Sugar was
introduced to the New World by Spain and Portugal, following their successful production of the crop on the island of Madeira and in the Canary Islands.
Christopher Columbus brought sugar to the Spanish colonies in America on his
second voyage in 1493 to Hispaniola. Portugal had developed extensive sugar plan-

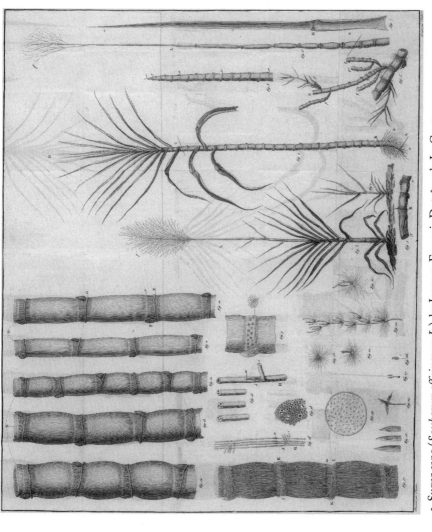

2. Sugar cane (*Saccharum officinarum L.*), by Jacques-François Dutrône de La Couture, 1790. (Courtesy of the John Carter Brown Library at Brown University)

tations in Brazil by the early 1600s. Soon after that, the English, French, and Dutch began to develop sugar plantations in their Caribbean colonies (Galloway 1989:50–78). Sugar was apparently produced on a small scale in Florida soon after St. Augustine was established in 1565; processing of the cane was probably conducted with hand-operated roller mills (Bathe 1955:105; Smith et al. 1994:21).

The New World plantations far surpassed those of the Mediterranean in production of sugar, to the point that by the eighteenth century, "sugar cane was the most important cash crop in tropical America, dominating the economies of several colonies and making an important contribution to the economic life of many more" (Galloway 1989:84). Sugar had "transitioned from a luxury good to a status approaching a staple. Production volumes contributed directly to price reductions as the market became glutted. Its distinction as a prerogative of the elite diminished, its use became more widespread, and production was further stimulated" (Meniketti 2006:76). In order to remain profitable, planters had to adopt innovations to reduce labor costs, improve yields, and mitigate both deforestation and soil exhaustion (Galloway 1989:84).

Growing Sugar

Sugar cane (Figure 2) "is a coarse grass, sometimes reaching heights of 20 ft., easily rooting from the nodes, and typically propagated . . . by cuttings" (Schery 1952:339). All varieties of sugar cane are part of the family of large grasses called *Poaceae* (Eubanks 1992:13). Historically the most important variety was the "noble cane," or *Saccharum officinarum,* which grows to a height of approximately 15 feet with a stalk approximately 2 inches thick. This relatively soft stalk has a high juice yield (Mintz 1985:21). Another popular variety, particularly in the North American colonies of Florida and Georgia, was known as "ribbon cane," which may have been either *Otaheite* (Tahiti or Bourbon cane) or a cold-resistant variety such as Batavian Striped or Black Java. All of these canes are more cold resistant than "noble cane," although *Otaheite* is susceptible to wind damage and disease (Galloway 1989:141).

Sugar cane stalks are cylindrical and divided into segments or joints from which the leaves grow. The thickness of the outer layer or rind of the stalk determines not only how resistant it is to disease and cold, but also how much juice it will hold and how easily this juice can be extracted by crushing the stalks (Eubanks 1992:14).

The plant grows extremely well in the rich black high-organic soils of lowlands. The resultant sugar grains are not as soft as those of other regions and there is less molasses than from lowland cane, both desirable results in terms of a marketable product (Sitterson 1953:122). Soil quality also affects the amount of sugar that the cane yields. Rich soils lead to very viscous cane juice which "often will not boil into sugar" (Long 1774:441–442). Thus the sandy soils of Florida might be expected to yield more juice. Other soil qualities that can affect the quality of the cane are its salt and nitrogen levels, acidity, and drainage (Smith 2005:42). As previously noted, the warm climate and freshwater swamps of the Halifax region were ideal for cane cultivation (Griffin 1999:17).

An early-nineteenth-century treatise written by East Florida sugar planter John C. Cleland states that the best soil should have a clay or marl foundation with eight inches of topsoil. Cleland states that "a kind of soapy clay, intermixed with alluvial soil, or sand and shells or black loomy mould, may be considered prime sugar land; sand alone, unless thoroughly cowpenned [manured], cannot produce a cane crop" (Cleland 1836:19). Bathe (1955:111) says that the ribbon cane, or *Otaheite*, favored in Florida could yield 2,000 pounds of sugar per acre, "but requires a great deal of fertilizing, and clay bottom lands are best for growing."

The asexually propagated cane was usually planted in rows approximately four to six feet apart, although in some of the Caribbean islands, a system of squares was used for soil conservation (Figure 3). In the West Indies today, intercropping with potatoes or other plants is sometimes practiced (Ceylon Barclay, president of Ormond Beach Historic Trust and former rum maker, personal communication 1999). During planting, "A furrow, or series of holes, is made, four or five inches deep, and two joints of cane put in side by side, so that in case one joint fails to germinate, the other may supply its place" (Olcott 1857:81). The joints were usually cuttings from the tops of mature stalks that had been stripped of their leaves. The new plants sprouted from the nodes at the joints of the seed cane, maturing within 9 to 18 months, depending upon the weather (Eubanks 1992:14, 16). In Georgia and Florida, planting was usually conducted in the fall during the active harvest season to avoid having to store seed cane over the winter (Sitterson 1953:122).

Cane will reproduce from the same joints for many years in succession, although the later "ratoon cane" may be less vigorous and produce less juice (Schery 1952:340; Eubanks 1992:16). However, one visitor to the Halifax River in East Florida claimed that a planter in that area got six years of cane of a consistent quality without replanting. He also noted that the top of the cane stalk was used as animal fodder and that the cane was thick enough to smother weeds (Williams 1837:106).

Once the cane fields were prepared and the crop planted, the crop required little attention beyond occasional weeding until harvest (Griffin 1999:18). Cleland (1836:20–21) recommended hoeing the fields once the canes appeared to be grassy in order to keep the roots free of interference. He also advocated a second hoeing once the canes were three to four feet high, removing the dry leaves and using them as mulch—he referred to this as "*trashing canes.*"

An early-nineteenth-century visitor to East Florida, John Lee Williams, indicated that one slave could tend 5 acres of cane (Williams 1837:106), while another account from the same period said that most plantations cultivated 150 to 200 acres with one slave for every 2 acres (Olcott 1857:78).

3. Planting sugar cane in Antigua, West Indies, by William Clark, 1833. (Courtesy of the John Carter Brown Library at Brown University)

Harvesting and processing the cane required the presence of all hands virtually around the clock. Cane was harvested in the fall during a short period between the time when it has ripened and the onset of cold weather. The cane cutters stripped the stalks of leaves, cut off unripened joints, and then severed the stalk at the roots with large cane knives (Figure 4). The cut stalks were gathered into bundles and carted to the mill for processing (Sitterson 1953:134). It was considered important to cut the canes as close to the ground surface as possible and keep them covered with cane leaves while carting to the mill (Cleland 1836:21).

Processing Sugar

The sugar mill and boiling house—sometimes with associated stables, bagasse house (to dry the pressed stalks), distillery, and slave quarters—were usually in proximity to the cane fields. The sugar works of the seventeenth and eighteenth centuries were simple affairs (Figure 5), consisting of a series of fire chambers with accompanying boiling kettles under a rudimentary roof. By the nineteenth century, "the mill or sugar house was the dominant building" on a sugar plantation (Vlach 1993:127). The complex included a mill for grinding the cane, the sugar house with its boilers and furnace, and the cooling vats of the purgery (Figure 6). Overall, the image was that of "a large machine shed punctuated by tall chimneys spewing smoke and venting steam" (Vlach 1993:127–128).

A month or so before harvest, the sugar works were overhauled and readied for production. This could include disassembly of the machinery, as well as thorough cleaning of the kettles, coolers, and tanks. It could also include whitewashing the building itself. As agricultural historian Henry Olcott described the process first-hand in the late nineteenth century, "In short, the sugar house has been in a state of slow fermentation since last crop, and must be sweetened by plentiful doses of lime and water, to render it fit for new operations" (Olcott 1857:83).

There are four major steps involved in processing raw sugar from cane. First the cane is crushed to extract juice. The juice is then clarified to remove dirt and other impurities. Then the clarified juice is boiled to evaporate water and form a thick syrup. Finally, when the syrup begins to granulate, it is transferred to containers to crystallize. Molasses is basically the syrup drained from these containers, which is either sold as a syrup or further processed into rum. In some cases, when the primary goal is production of molasses, the boiling process is stopped before granulation (Eubanks 1992:17).

Milling Sugar Cane

Prior to the early seventeenth century, sugar was milled using systems adapted from processing flour, olive oil, and grapes. An upright wheel with a horizontal

4. Harvesting sugar cane in Antigua, West Indies, by William Clark, 1833. (Courtesy of the John Carter Brown Library at Brown University)

1. Moulin. 2. Fourneaux. 3. Formes. 4. Vinaigrerie. 5. Cannes *SVCRERIE* 6. Gros 7. Latanir. 8. Pasomirioba 9. Choux 10. Cases 11. Figuir. 177.
de Sucre. Cocos. 115. P. 111. Caraïbes. de Negres P. 92.
le Chien 1.

5. Seventeenth-century sugar works in the Antilles, by Jean Baptiste DuTertre, 1667. (Courtesy of the John Carter Brown Library at Brown University)

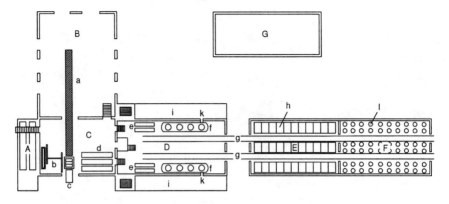

A Boilers, B Cane Shed, C Mill House, D Boiling House,
E Cooling House, F Purgery, G Distillery

a Cane Carrier, b Mill and Engine, c Bagasse Shute, d Juice Tanks,
e Defecators, f Trains, g Rails to carry syrup to coolers and sugar to purgery,
h Coolers, i Alley ways, k Furnace Mouths, l Sugar Hogsheads

6. Idealized ground plan for sugar works, based on Henry S. Olcott, 1857.

drive shaft turned in a depression into which the cane was placed. The pressed cane was then re-pressed using a beam or screw press (Galloway 1989:37). By 1600, the vertical mill had been adopted throughout most of the New World. This mill consisted of a set of three vertical wooden rollers with a drive shaft at the top (Mintz 1985:27–28; cf. Figure 7). The cylinders were usually 30 to 40 inches long and 20 to 25 inches in diameter with gears at the top. The moving power was applied to the middle cylinder. As the mills developed, the surfaces of the wooden cylinders were fluted to better grip and crush the cane. A plate at the base formed a pan to catch the juice, which would then be channeled through a trough or tubes to the boiling kettles. Early mills were usually animal powered, using as many as four pairs of oxen, horses, or mules (Griffin 1999:19; Sitterson 1953:138). The cane was fed between the primary feed rollers and sometimes returned through the secondary rollers to increase the amount of juice extracted. Alternatively the mill could be fed from two sides resulting in a single crushing (Eubanks 1992:17). Later the wooden rollers were sheathed with iron, and by the mid-eighteenth century wooden rollers were replaced by rollers made completely of cast iron (Figure 8). It wasn't until the late eighteenth century that more efficient horizontal mills (Figure 9), often steam powered, were introduced (Eubanks 1992:19). These rollers were generally cast iron; planter Thomas Spalding of Georgia stated that they cost 8½¢ per pound from M'Queen's Foundry in Savannah (Spalding 1816:238). The three horizontal rollers were "brought very close together by means of large screws fixed in the iron frame for that purpose" (Olcott 1857:85). The first and second rollers were spaced

7. Animal-powered vertical sugar mill, by Philippe Fermin, 1770. (Courtesy of the John Carter Brown Library at Brown University)

about ⅛ to 3⁄16 inch apart, while the second and third rollers were approximately a knife blade's thickness apart. As the cane passed through the rollers, the juice ran into a pan under the rollers, and then through a channel to the clarifiers. In some cases, it was pumped into a receiver and then redistributed to the clarifier and kettles (Olcott 1857:86). The crushed cane stalks (bagasse) were discarded or used as animal feed until the 1850s, when they began to be used as a fuel in steam-powered mills (Sitterson 1953:140).

Another innovation introduced with horizontal mills was the cane carrier (Figure 9). The carrier was "an endless chain, carrying a series of slats, or boards, leading direct to the feed-board of the mill, and moving on rollers with the motion of the machine, but so arranged as to be stopped when required, independent of the mill" (Olcott 1857:84–85).

It should be noted that as early as 1807, Oliver Evans of Philadelphia advertised that he could "execute such orders as he may receive, either for steam engines or mill work, sugar boilers, kettles or kerbs, rollers for sugar mills, which may be

8. Williams animal-powered horizontal sugar mill.

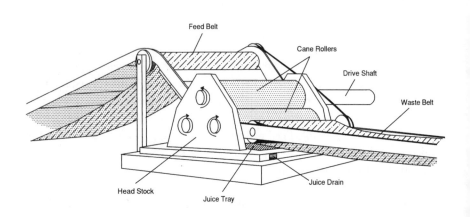

Feed Belt

Cane Rollers

Drive Shaft

Waste Belt

Head Stock

Juice Tray

Juice Drain

Horizontal Cane Mill

9. Steam-powered horizontal sugar cane mill and cane carrier, based on Henry S. Olcott, 1857.

neatly turned and finished" (Bathe 1955:107). Clearly steam-powered mills were readily available by the beginning of the nineteenth century. A study of the adaptation of the Boulton and Watt stationary steam engine in Jamaica stated that during the period between 1803 and 1833, sales of these engines to Caribbean sugar planters were exceeded only by sales to the cotton industry (Satchell 2002:242–243). Steam engines were more reliable than wind power, produced more constant speed than animals, reduced uneven wear on the rollers, and were more efficient in extracting juice from the cane. They also could be operated with bagasse as fuel (Satchell 2002:246–247). As Henry Nelson Coleridge noted in 1825: "Surely where water and coals may be commanded, the certainty and rapidity of making sugar would in the long run be worth the additional expense" of a steam engine (qtd. in Meniketti 2006:59). It should be noted, however, that steam-powered mills did not reduce labor requirements or provide a significant increase in speed of crushing; what they primarily offered was constant availability of power and increased crushing power (Meniketti 2006:62–63).

Steam power also introduced a new requirement to sugar works—chimneys, sometimes one for the engine and one for the sugar train. According to Olcott, the chimney was the most important part of a sugar works: "If this should be too small, or should not draw properly, it puts a stop to everything. Steam cannot be got up in the boilers, therefore the mill cannot work; the sugar trains only partially boil, and general consternation prevails" (Olcott 1857:82). This explains the massive chimneys that dominate the various sugar works built after the Jamaica train and steam power were introduced.

The early animal-powered mills were usually adjacent to the boiling house. At later sugar works the mill was often separate from the boiling house, with a trough used to drain the juice from the mill to the boiling house. Whenever possible, mills were placed at a higher elevation but close to the boiling house, so that the juice could be transferred by gravity feed from mill to boiling train (Meniketti 2006:64).

Boiling the Cane Juice

Although initially a single room consisting of a roofed shed over the boiling kettles, later sugar houses consisted of two rooms, one for boiling and one for purging the raw sugar. Cleland (1836:22) advocated a 40- by 60-foot boiling house and curing house with an attached shed for cooling.

Close to the mill at one end of the boiling house was an area known as the clarifier or defecator (see Figure 6e), where the extracted juice was carried "by a spout into two or more large vats, usually shallow, rectangular boxes of cypress plank, holding many hundreds of gallons" (Sitterson 1953:140). By the nineteenth century these vats were lined with copper or lead. The vats began the first stage of sugar making, clarification. This process could include screening the juice or draining the juice from vat to vat with a copper tube, leaving impurities in the bottom of the first vat. Impurities included pith, rind, wax, and dissolved albuminous or gummy matters (Sitterson 1953:140).

An 1836 publication by sugar planter John C. Cleland described this process in East Florida. The first step was to test the pressed juice using a saccharometer, which is a graduated instrument to measure the amount of sugar in the juice. The juice was then transferred to the clarifier which was gently heated. A small amount of juice was then mixed with alkali or ground lime and added to the clarifier. This "tempering" hastened the precipitation of trash in the juice. After 10 or 15 minutes, a thick, mucous coat formed on the surface. When the coat began to crack and bubble, the heat was removed and the juice was passed into the kettles, filling each to about two-thirds. The fires were then started and boiling began (Cleland 1836:31–32).

The next step was boiling. Although initially a single iron kettle and furnace were used for boiling, the process eventually changed to a series of kettles. Four kettles required a space about 30 feet long and 7 or 8 feet wide, with the tops of the kettles set about 2½ feet above the floor (Sitterson 1953:141). A set of kettles ranged in size from the largest at 52 to 72 inches in diameter to the smallest at 33 to 54 inches in diameter. In order, from largest at the mill end to smallest, the four kettles were named *grande, flambeau, sirop,* and *battèrie* (Sitterson 1953:141). When five kettles were used, the second kettle was named the *propre.* Often, the final strike pan was called the *teche,* or teach, rather than *battèrie.* The French terms are commonly used today when describing sugar trains. Archaeologist Thomas Eubanks (1992:30) states that in the nineteenth century there were seven- and nine-kettle trains in operation in the West Indies; however, this practice was not present in the East Florida region. Cleland (1836:29) indicates that the larger kettles were usually cast iron, but the *teche* was always copper.

At first each kettle continued to have a separate furnace in a format known as the "Spanish train" (Figure 10), but later an arrangement called a "Jamaica train" or "French train" was established that used a single furnace for all of the kettles (Eubanks 1992:30; see also Figure 11). While the Spanish train was believed to produce better sugar, it required more fuel than the more efficient Jamaica train (Payne and Griffin 2001:21). In this study, only Oswald/Yonge's Three Chimneys and McHardy definitely had a Spanish train, although the earliest part of Dunlawton may also have originated as a Spanish train. The remaining sites discussed in this book used the Jamaica train. Since fuel was not an issue in Florida due to the abundant forests, the Jamaica train was adopted for its efficiency in processing large amounts of juice—and probably also because it was the process current at the time the later sugar works were erected.

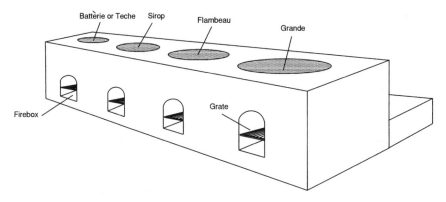

Spanish Train

10. Spanish sugar train, based on Jean Baptiste DuTertre, 1667.

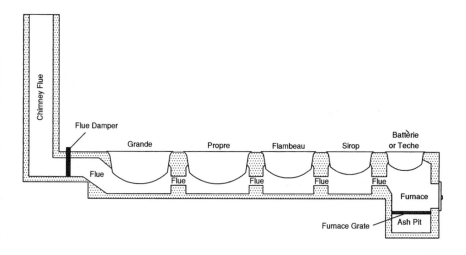

Jamaica Train

11. Jamaica sugar train, based on Henry S. Olcott, 1857.

When the single-furnace Jamaica train system (Figure 11) was adopted, the furnace was placed farthest from the *grande* under the strike pan (*battèrie* or *teche*), thus placing the most heat under the final kettle (Eubanks 1992:30). The single-furnace system used a flue under the kettles and a chimney that was located at the *grande* end of the train where the flue made a right-angle turn into the chimney (Sitterson 1953:141). The furnace mouth at the opposite end of the train was marked by grate bars, an ash pit, and perhaps doors. In order to have the kettles approximately 24 to 30 inches above the floor (reasonable working height), the furnace was placed essentially underground or in an area excavated beneath the side of the boiling house (Olcott 1857:88). A platform adjacent to the train allowed workers to skim off impurities from the kettles.

The cast-iron kettles were set so that the supporting masonry increased their capacity by rising several inches above the kettle rims; later a copper lining formed a gutter around the kettle rim (Sitterson 1953:141; Olcott 1857:90–91). Writer Henry Olcott (1857:90) said the second pan was set approximately two inches higher than the first so that if it overflowed during boiling, it would spill back into the first pan. The copper gutter had an opening that led to an overflow or "scum" kettle located next to the train. The overflow was then returned to the clarifiers after settling. The copper collars also contained the froth from the boiling process. The final strike kettle also had a copper collar to channel overflows back into the preceding kettle. After the kettles were set in the masonry, the train was covered with a board surface with openings for the kettles. This surface was covered with sheet copper and slanted to carry boil-overs back to the initial vessel. In more sophisticated trains, a lead- or copper-lined juice receiver was located adjacent to or over the clarifiers, with a moveable trough or pipes to deliver juice to the desired kettles (Olcott 1857:91).

At the beginning of the sugar-making process, the *grande* was filled from the clarifier, and between 6 and 24 inches of slaked lime (a mix of lime and water, which reduces the lime to calcium hydroxide) was mixed with two to three gallons of juice or water to form a milky liquid. This milk was stirred into the juice in the *grande* in order to neutralize the acid in the juice and improve coagulation of impurities. At times, egg whites or cattle blood was also used for coagulation (Smith 2005:43). As the juice heated, a thick scum formed on the surface. When a watery vapor began to come through the scum, the kettle was skimmed using shallow 10- to 12-inch-wide skimmers, often copper, on long wooden handles (Figure 12). The scum was thrown into an adjacent vat and carried outside via a gutter. Froth remaining in the kettle was beaten down into the juice. After skimming, the juice was considered clarified and was transferred into the next kettles, the *propre, flambeau,* and *sirop.* As these kettles began to boil, additional scum formed and was pushed back into the preceding kettle. As the volume of liquid was reduced, the kettles were refilled by bailing from kettle to kettle and refilling the *grande* with a new batch of juice. Bailing was done using wooden five- to eight-gallon buckets on handles 9 to 10 feet long supported by a hook on a beam parallel to the train. The whole operation was conducted by only the most experienced slaves and the sugar master, who may have been an overseer or the owner (Olcott 1857:95–96; Sitterson 1953:141–142; Griffin 1999:19).

Once the syrup in the strike pan (*teche* or *battèrie*) reached a golden color and ceased to froth or bubble, it was ready to be transferred to the cooler. To test for granulation, a large copper spoon with a wooden handle was dipped into the strike

12. Boiling sugar and sugar cones, by M. Chambon, 1783. (Courtesy of the John Carter Brown Library at Brown University)

pan. If the syrup on the spoon thickly covered the surface, drained slowly, and had a grainy appearance, it was ready to transfer. The whole process required one to two hours depending on the sugar quality of the juice and the efficiency of the facilities themselves (Sitterson 1953:143). Cleland again provided a good description of the final stages of sugar manufacture. Once evaporation ceased and the liquid was reduced to a thick syrup, the temperature was monitored until it reached 232 to 240 degrees. The fires were then damped, and the thick sugar syrup was ladled into a gutter that carried it to the coolers (Cleland 1836:32–33).

It should be noted that one advance in sugar boiling in the early nineteenth century never appears to have been adopted in Florida. By the 1830s, Louisiana sugar works were using vacuum pans for boiling sugar. This method was faster and produced a higher-quality sugar. Soon after their introduction, a New Orleans free African-American engineer named Norbert Rillieux developed the multiple-effect evaporation system, which linked a series of vacuum pans so that each vessel was heated by the vapor from the previous vessel. This was a significant step in reducing fuel consumption, as well as faster processing (Mullenix 2007:6). In combination with centrifuges to remove molasses, this method doubled the amount of sugar produced by the traditional systems used in East Florida (Smith 2005:217).

Cooling and Purging

Coolers were oblong wooden troughs approximately 5 by 10 feet and 10 to 12 inches deep (Figure 13). "They are set parallel with the train in a double row, six in each

13. Sugar boiling house in Antigua, West Indies, by William Clark, 1833 (note coolers on the right). (Courtesy of the John Carter Brown Library at Brown University)

row" (Olcott 1857:97). The coolers were loaded in three to four sequential "strikes" of three to four inches in depth from the *battèrie* or *teche*, with a brief cooling period between each strike to allow crystallization to begin. While cooling, the liquid was agitated in the troughs to spread the crystals uniformly throughout the syrup.

After 6 to 14 hours, the crystallizing sugar was dug out of the coolers and placed in copper basins or tubs to be transferred to hogsheads in the purging house (Sitterson 1953:143; Olcott 1857:98; Gluckman and Baker 1967:9). A contemporary description states that if the sugar hardened, it needed to be gently chopped up so that no large lumps were put in the barrels. The sugar was packed into the barrels evenly and pressed down. If done properly, the sugar would not sink or break up, firming within an hour or so. It then cured (drained) for about three weeks (Roughley 1823:262–263).

The purging house essentially consisted of a draining room 40 to 60 feet long with a floor of boards separated by about a foot. Molasses cisterns 16 to 20 inches deep were located under the floor within an area of about 20 square feet. Cleland (1836:22–23) and Spalding (1816:243) each describe a building with slanting floors funneling the molasses into a gutter that led to the cisterns (Figure 14). Spalding described the curing house as having joists spaced at 15 inches, with the gutter also inclining toward a closed cistern at one end. This cistern would hold about 2,000 gallons and could be made of wood lined with clay. The cistern enclosure kept the molasses clear. He also recommended a plank walkway between the casks for ease of transfer (Spalding 1816:243). These cisterns were usually cypress as Spalding states, but could also be stuccoed brick or tabby (a form of concrete common in the southeastern United States made from lime from burned shells, sand, and water). Cleland (1836:24) says that wooden cisterns were lead lined. If level, the cisterns needed a pump to transfer the molasses to kegs; if on a slope, a cock could be used.

At this point, the sugar was a brown mixture of approximately 60 percent sugar and 40 percent molasses. Empty wooden hogsheads with open joints were placed on the board floor; the lower part of the barrels had three or four auger holes plugged with sugar canes on the interior that extended almost to the top of the barrel. The crystallized sugar was placed in the tubs and allowed to drain for two to three days while the purging house was kept warm. The plugs were then removed from the hogsheads, and the barrels were allowed to drain for 20 to 30 days, resulting in 40 to 45 gallons of molasses. During this period the hogsheads were continually filled until they contained only sugar, totaling approximately 1,000 pounds. At that point the barrels were sealed for shipment (Olcott 1857:98; Sitterson 1953:144). The molasses was also collected and shipped, or used for making rum.

An alternate purging process was known as claying. In this process conical metal or ceramic molds (see Figure 12 and Loftfield 2001:221–224) were placed in wooden frames or large ceramic pots in the purging house. Small holes in the bottom were

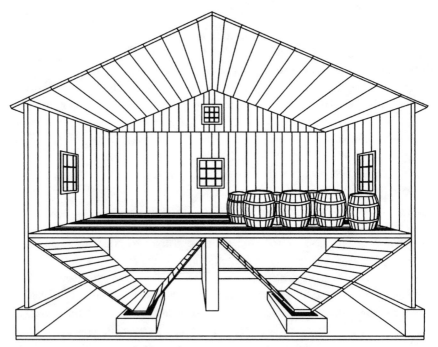

14. Sugar purgery or curing house, based on John C. Cleland, 1836.

plugged, again using cane. As with the barrel method, the sugar was placed in the molds and after a day or two the plug was removed. At that time a thin, creamy clay and water paste was poured on top of the sugar in the mold. Water was then poured over the clay and allowed to percolate through the sugar, washing out the molasses and leaving a much whiter sugar crystal than the hogshead method. Claying was sometimes repeated two or three times to improve the whiteness by decreasing the molasses content. The resulting cones of sugar graded from white to yellow to brown at the tip with a molasses/sugar mix at the extreme tip. After unmolding, the cones were broken by color, crushed, and dried on hot tile floors or boards in the sun. The resulting powdered sugar was packed into boxes held together with dried rawhide (Olcott 1857:100). This lighter sugar was easier to refine, and the process yielded more molasses, which could be made into rum (Smith 2005:50–51).

The end products of the sugar-making process were sugar, molasses, and bagasse. The molasses was consumed as syrup, used in cattle feed, or further processed into rum or vinegar (Schery 1952:341). In East Florida, rum was a secondary by-product of sugar production, with the amount of rum produced based on the current sugar market, the amount of rum required as legal tender for participation in the slave trade, and the amount needed on the plantation itself, where it was often doled out to laborers as an incentive to production (Griffin 1999:18–19).

It was not an export product, since only small quantities were produced. Only Oswald/Yonge's Three Chimneys and Dummett in this study have structural evidence of rum making.

Cane into Rum

Molasses and/or cane juice were turned into rum by fermenting, distilling, coloring, and aging the results. Several methods of fermentation could be used. The simplest method, used only at harvest time, consisted of using pure cane juice from the mill rather than molasses. This method required no additives since the juice contained a mild airborne strain of yeast (Payne 1995:17; Barclay 1994:42). Another method, employed when sugar was actively being produced, used all the skimmings from the sugar process mixed with molasses. Alternatively, the molasses was placed in a large vat or tank where yeast was added. Wash (skimmings and water) and dunder (residue from previous distillations) were also added to this tank. A final method used a mix of one part molasses and five parts water, sometimes with *cush-cush*, the fine bagasse particles retrieved by the initial straining of the cane juice. *Cush-cush* functioned as a yeast. Some type of acid and lime or vegetable ash were also added to the mix. In all methods alcohol vapor and carbonic acid were produced as the yeast consumed the liquid sugar (Eubanks 1992:32). This process works best at an optimum temperature of 780 degrees Fahrenheit (Barclay 1994:121). After approximately six days of fermentation this alcohol-enriched syrup, also called wash, was transferred to a still for further processing (Barclay 1994:121; Eubanks 1992:32).

The quality of the mix determined the alcohol content of the resulting rum (Smith 2005:45). The particular combination used for the wash varied from plantation to plantation and was often a carefully guarded secret. But a planter in Jamaica described two variations in 1794. One mix of 100 gallons of wash contained equal parts of scum, dunder, and water, with molasses added in 3-gallon amounts after the first day and again a day or two later. His second, improved mix used 50 gallons of dunder, 6 gallons of molasses, 36 gallons of scum, and 8 gallons of water (Smith 2005:45). Distillers recognized that the sugar level was critical to fermentation; thus the mix was varied through the season based on the amount of molasses available (Smith 2005:46). The length of fermentation time also affected the end product. Two weeks was considered optimum; a relatively slow fermentation could be obtained by adding cold water to the mix (Smith 2005:46). Humidity also affected the process. Fermentation works best in dry conditions, since as alcohol absorbs water, the temperature falls and fermentation slows. In order to keep the still house dry, small fires could be lit (Smith 2005:42–43).

The still itself consisted of a pot still; a doubler, or retort; and a series of metal coils called the worm (generally pewter) which were submerged in a tank of cold

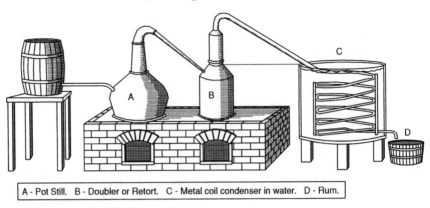

A - Pot Still.   B - Doubler or Retort.   C - Metal coil condenser in water.   D - Rum.

Distillery

15. Rum distillery, based on Florence Lewisohn, 1964.

water called a worm pipe (Figure 15). Submersion of the coils cooled the vapors, promoting condensation (Barclay 1994:122). The pot still was filled with the fermented wash, while the doubler was filled to about one-quarter with low wine—a weak, low-proof rum (less than 108 proof). Low wine was obtained at either the beginning or end of distillation. The two containers were connected by a gooseneck pipe and sat on fireboxes. As the wash or mash began to cook, vapors passed through the gooseneck into the doubler via a pipe, which reached within two to three inches of the bottom of the vessel. These hot gases caused the low wine to boil, generating higher-proof gases which passed into the metal cooling coils. There the vapor condensed into rum, which was drained through the exit pipe into a wooden tub (Lewisohn 1964:36–37).

The captured rum could then be colored, if desired, and the proof sometimes adjusted by the addition of water. The completed mix was placed in barrels or casks called puncheons to age; these barrels held about 110 to 150 wine gallons. Rum directly from the still ranged between 130 to 150 proof (Eubanks 1992:32; Lewisohn 1964:36–37; Barclay 1994:122). A 1,000-gallon still yielded approximately 500 gallons of rum in a 15-hour period (Wray 1848:408). Of that, the initial five gallons was saved as low wine. As the process continued, the proof dropped to 108; this final draw was also saved as low wine (Lewisohn 1964:36–37).

In some cases, the rum was sold directly from the still without further aging, but the normal practice would be to transfer the raw rum to oak casks where it would be aged for two to four years. This results in a mellower product, which could then be sold by the barrel or bottled (Barclay 1994:122). At times the rum was also redistilled to remove more impurities, improve the taste, and yield a higher proof (Smith 2005:47).

4
Sugar in East Florida

The planter may expect with some hope of success, to reap from his labors,
an abundant and lucrative harvest.

—John C. Cleland, *The Superior Advantages to Be Derived
from the Culture of Sugar-Cane, in East-Florida* (1836)

Was sugar lucrative in East Florida? The short answer to this question is that by
and large, sugar was not a profitable product in East Florida. But that does not
mean it didn't have the potential to be a moneymaking endeavor. A number of
factors limited this potential in East Florida, perhaps chief among them a series
of wars that affected not only who controlled the territory but also what was hap-
pening to the occupants.

First Spanish Period, 1565 to 1763

Although Florida was explored as early as 1513 by Juan Ponce de León, the first
permanent settlement was established at St. Augustine in 1565 by Pedro Menén-
dez de Avilés (Gannon 2003:4). Spain claimed a much larger area than present-day
Florida, but made only limited efforts to settle it. They did establish a chain of missions across the territory from St. Augustine to present-day Tallahassee, and north
along the coast of Georgia. There was also a thriving cattle ranch in North Central Florida on Paynes Prairie in what is now Alachua County. But their agricultural pursuits were largely unsuccessful, and the initial Spanish colony was depen-
dent on money and supplies from the homeland (Gannon 2003:4–14).

During the First Spanish Period, Florida was not a major source of agricultural products. As anthropologist Patricia Griffin says, "agriculture was rudimentary, taking a back seat to the position of St. Augustine as a garrison town. For
these early European conquerors of the Americas, the extraction of precious met-
als, such as gold and silver, was the principal aim" (Griffin 2003:163). Although the
Spaniards introduced sugar cane to Florida, it was probably grown only as a product for local consumption (Cresap 1982:153).

Sugar was a major export from the Americas during this period, but it came
from Brazil and the Caribbean, not North America. In fact, "sugar became so vital
to national economies [of Europe] during the 18th century that empires bitterly

fought for sugar islands and willingly ceded continental land to maintain their grip on Caribbean real estate" (Meniketti 2006:53). But these sugar centers did not include Spanish Florida.

One activity that would ultimately have a disastrous effect on the sugar plantations of East Florida began in the early eighteenth century. Partly in reaction to the hostility of the British colonies on its borders, Spain began to encourage Creek Indians from Georgia and Alabama to migrate to Florida. There they would become known as the Seminole. The Spanish settlers traded with the Seminole but largely left them alone in the interior of the territory. The Seminole and the Spanish government also offered a refuge to escaped slaves from the British colonies. If the slaves were willing to become Catholic, Spain would allow them to settle as freed men in the Florida colony.

During the French and Indian War of 1754 to 1763, Spain sided with France in 1761. After England seized Havana, Cuba, Spain was forced by the Treaty of Paris in 1763 to give England control of the colonies east of the Mississippi River, including Louisiana and Florida (Gannon 2003:17). Spanish landowners could sell out and move to the Spanish colony in Cuba or remain under British control. Many of the landowners opted to leave, so the never large white population was decreased even more.

British Period, 1763 to 1783

As noted earlier in this book, the British established two colonies, East and West Florida, with capitals in St. Augustine and Pensacola, respectively. When the British acquired Florida in 1763, they immediately began making a series of large land grants specifically to develop plantations to produce cash crops. Of course, it was also hoped that these grants would replace the departed Spanish population. This was a settlement pattern that had been highly successful in the southern American colonies to the north of Florida, and in the British Caribbean, and there was every reason to expect that it could be implemented in the new Florida colony.

Based on the success and profitability of sugar in the Caribbean colonies, the British felt that subtropical Florida would also be good sugar country. The British had the added benefit of people with experience in both growing and processing sugar cane who could be brought to Florida. In addition, the new British colony, like those colonies to the north, was more than willing to operate its sugar plantations with slave labor.

But things did not go as smoothly as the British had expected. Although the virtues of Florida were extolled in publications, there were not many takers. One exception was a group of wealthy London businessmen who were members of the East Florida Society of London. These men used their connections to obtain large grants in Florida, not realizing how difficult and expensive it would be to develop these tracts (Schafer 1982:37).

Two of the largest attempts to settle grants were at Rollestown on the St. Johns River across from present-day Palatka, Florida, and at New Smyrna on the coast south of St. Augustine. Denys Rolles established his settlement with a mix of vagrants, debtors, and beggars from London—hardly the stuff of successful plantations (Fabel 1996:141). Andrew Turnbull fared little better with his New Smyrna colony. He imported settlers from British-controlled Minorca as indentured servants, but treated them harshly. As a result, after nine years, his settlers fled to St. Augustine, abandoning the fledgling New Smyrna colony (Gannon 2003:20–21). Thus, even with the support and encouragement of Florida governor James Grant, the ill-fated colonies in New Smyrna and Rollestown failed within 10 years of the British acquisition of Florida (Griffin 2003:164–165). It should be noted, however, that Turnbull did experiment with sugar at New Smyrna, even hiring William Forbes, an experienced sugar planter from Jamaica. Near the end of his colony, he talked of planting more than 3,000 acres in sugar cane and building a mill, if the indigo crop (his primary focus) was sufficiently profitable (Schafer 2008). Writer John Forbes visited the abandoned settlement in 1821 and described "stacks of chimneys, some boilers, and other traces of the sugar works, and some wells of most excellent water" (qtd. in Floyd 1937:90).

Individual plantations fared somewhat better, particularly those that produced indigo. Governor Grant sought the advice of long-time friends among the South Carolina planters, and induced several of them to assume grants in Florida, including the Moultrie brothers (Schafer 1982:38). One of the best-documented attempts at sugar production in East Florida was that of another of Governor Grant's friends, London merchant Richard Oswald. In fact, the governor essentially supervised Oswald's grant, since Oswald never came to Florida.

Oswald divided his 20,000-acre grant into several distinct settlements, each with a specific purpose. One of these, the Swamp Settlement in what is today Ormond Beach, was designated as a sugar plantation. Oswald imported a Jamaican planter experienced with sugar to oversee and operate the Swamp Settlement. Unfortunately, the effort was unsuccessful and the property was abandoned before 1781 or 1782, based on several descriptions from that period (Payne and Griffin 2001:35). One visitor, Lt. Col. John Douglas, stated "That this Situation was too far to the Northward for a Sugar Plantation & [Douglas] has heard that the plan not succeeding, was laid aside on that Account" (Douglas 1786).

Other planters in East Florida experimented with sugar during the British Period, including Robert McHardy, Lieutenant Governor John Moultrie, and William Elliot (Payne and Griffin 2001:3, 7; Griffin 1999:Table 1).

While thousands of pounds of sugar were being exported from the Caribbean islands and Brazil during the eighteenth century, "The cultivation of sugar [in

East Florida], from which much had been hoped for, never got beyond the experimental stage and suffered from occasional frosts" (Mowat 1964:78). Archaeologist Ted Payne and anthropologist Patricia Griffin (Payne and Griffin 2001:7) have noted that this period encompassed a time of "freak weather" that was colder than the norm for Florida. Sugar also had to compete with indigo, which commanded high prices throughout the British Period (Payne and Griffin 2001:7). The short duration of British control may also be a factor; 20 years may not have been long enough to develop a successful sugar plantation system in East Florida. As one writer has said: "Sugar mills left behind by the British were also remnants of dreams rather than reality. Production of this staple apparently never emerged from the experimental stage. The sugar produced was locally consumed and even then local production never seems to have satisfied the demand" (Daniel et al. 1980:104).

In 1776, war again played a role in Florida's history. When the Revolutionary War broke out in the original 13 colonies to the north, the British managed to retain control of Florida, which became a haven for Tories from South Carolina and Georgia. In 1779, Spain entered the war on the side of the Americans, seizing West Florida in 1781. When the Treaty of Paris was negotiated in 1783, Britain ceded Florida back to Spain (Gannon 2003:24).

Second Spanish Period, 1783 to 1819

After the Spaniards regained Florida, they made the decision to continue the British plantation and land grant system. By the late eighteenth century, sugar plantations in Louisiana and parts of Texas had demonstrated that the crop was economically successful in the southernmost regions of North America (Eubanks 1985:24). Thus began the first major attempt to produce sugar on a large scale in East Florida.

The Florida planters were influenced not only by the successful plantations of the Caribbean, but also by sugar planting in coastal Georgia and South Carolina. Georgia sugar planter Thomas Spalding claimed that "The plantations at the mouth of the Altamaha [River in coastal Georgia] have been a source from whence the Cane plants have spread into the interior country of Georgia, and into Florida, every acre in Florida has been derived from that source" (qtd. in Floyd 1937:92). Spalding himself began planting sugar in 1805 and earned $12,500 from his 1814 crop. He also pioneered construction of large sugar works from tabby, a concrete made of lime from burned oyster shells, shells, sand, and water (Floyd 1937:91, 97).

Unfortunately for East Florida, several factors again led to limited success for the planters. By the time that the East Florida planters were building sugar works and experimenting with growth and production in the late eighteenth to early nineteenth century, Louisiana had already moved to a much larger scale of sugar plantation than those in East Florida would ever be. In 1797, more than 550,000 pounds of sugar were being shipped out of New Orleans, and by 1801, there were 75 sugar mills operating in Louisiana (Mullenix 2007:2). Sugar was still a major export from the Caribbean (particularly Cuba) and Brazil at this time. This is amply demonstrated by a review of records of foodstuffs imported into St. Augustine during the late eighteenth and early nineteenth centuries. In 1787, over 40,000 *reales* (monetary value) of sugar were imported from Havana. This had grown to over 48,000 *reales* in 1794 and over 100,000 *reales* in 1803 (Cusick 2000:180). Clearly, Spanish Florida was not producing sufficient sugar to satisfy its own needs during the early Second Spanish Period.

Establishment of a successful sugar plantation required more than the right soils and climate. As previously noted, "A sugar plantation was a large agro-industrial enterprise that took a good deal of capital to fund and a good deal of experience to manage profitably" (Galloway 1989:88). In addition to the land itself, which was in plentiful supply in East Florida, a planter needed slaves, mills, boiling and curing houses, accommodations for all concerned, agricultural implements, draft animals, and sufficient capital to support all of this for two years until the first crop could be harvested and processed (Galloway 1989:88).

All of this occurred during a period of already established and thriving competition and dropping sugar prices. One study reports that between 1813 and 1830, sugar fell from 57 shillings per hundredweight to 23 shillings per hundredweight (Satchell 2002:254). Bathe (1955:107) claims that the peak sugar prices in the South were reached by 1814, when Georgia sugar was listed at $12 to $14 per hundredweight, molasses at 60¢ to 70¢ per gallon and rum at $1.37 to $1.43 per gallon.

It should be noted that the East Florida planters were more optimistic about the cost-benefit ratio of sugar cane. Historian John Lee Williams wrote: "A general opinion has prevailed that sugar could not be made to advantage, unless a great capital is invested; but experience abundantly proves, that a small capital may be as profitably employed in the culture of cane, as any other product" (Williams 1837:106). Williams stated that 1,200 pounds of cane to the acre was a common yield in East Florida, concluding that "This at 7 dollars per hundred, amounts to 420 dollars for five acres. The molasses is always expected to pay the expense of manufacturing. Fifty acres of cane, well managed, will produce 4200 dollars; certainly the most profitable crop that can be raised in any part of the United States" (Williams 1837:106). The sense was that cane required less attention than other crops during the growing season, allowing workers to cultivate other crops and conduct plantation maintenance (Bishop 1975:5).

East Florida sugar planter John Cleland, writing in 1836, provided cost estimates for a 1,000-acre plantation in an optimum location. He based his estimate on cultivation of 100 acres of sugar cane by 40 slaves, 20 of whom were prime hands (healthy adults). The cost for purchase of the property, slaves, and equipment was placed at $51,000 with the proceeds in sugar and rum averaging $18,000 per year in the Charleston, South Carolina, market. From these proceeds, $1,030 would be taken in shipping charges and commissions and $2,000 would be paid out in annual plantation expenses such as salaries for the overseer, sugar maker, and distiller; clothing, food, and medical care for the slaves; taxes; and so on. The net proceeds would thus be $14,370, which Cleland indicated was an annual return of 27.5 percent on the invested capital (Cleland 1836:43–44).

Cleland based his initial costs on use of an animal-powered mill and construction of frame sugar works buildings. Steam-powered mills would cost at least $4,500(Sitterson 1953:138), while the masonry structures present at most of the sites in this study would require substantially more labor and expertise than frame buildings. Cleland also made no provisions for other plantation structures, including housing, barns, or outbuildings (Payne and Griffin 2001:30). Comparable structures at Dunlawton were valued at $1,450 in the 1830s (Strickland 1985:37). Thus Cleland's rate of return is highly optimistic and skewed. Other sources place the average annual rate of return for sugar in the early nineteenth century at 8 percent (Galloway 1989:89), while Cleland (1836:44) claimed Louisiana planters had been realizing 3 percent per year since 1829. Overall, it was a period of new technologies, often expensive, with declining revenues from sugar.

The competition, low prices for sugar, and low rate of return did not deter planters in East Florida from attempting to produce sugar during the Second Spanish Period. Griffin (1999:Table 1) identifies six sugar planters in the region during the period. By the early nineteenth century, indigo was no longer the favored crop for plantations; it had been surpassed by cotton, particularly the very valuable, long-staple Sea Island cotton. Sugar remained an experimental product for East Florida planters (Payne and Griffin 2001:8).

Attempts at producing sugar—or, for that matter, any other cash crop—in East Florida during the Second Spanish Period were further hampered by Indian unrest and the Patriot War of 1812, which forced many planters to abandon their properties for the safety of St. Augustine (Payne and Griffin 2001:8–9). Both Britain and Spain had maintained trading relations with the Seminole, leaving them mostly alone in the center and northern part of the territory. But harboring of runaway slaves by the Seminole continued to cause friction with the American states to the north, resulting in raiding parties into Florida. When the War of 1812 broke out between England and the United States, some of the American planters took advantage of this activity to raid East Florida during the so-called Patriot War, destroying plantations and crops (Coker and Parker 1996:163). Even after the Patriot War ended in 1814, unrest continued among the Seminole, culminating in the First Seminole War in 1818. This war led to the takeover of Florida by the United States through the Adams-Onis Treaty of 1819, in return for assumption of

Spain's debts to Americans and surrender of all American claims to Texas (Gannon 2003:27–28).

The Territorial Period, 1819 to 1835

To the new American government, Florida was a land ripe for expansion of the plantation system. This, of course, included solving the Indian problem by forcing them off their lands. One of the first acts of the new government was to negotiate a treaty with the Indians to get them out of the prime agricultural lands of North Florida and the coastal areas. The 1823 Treaty of Moultrie Creek confined the Indians to an area extending south of Ocala in Central Florida to Charlotte Harbor in South Florida, but 20 miles inland from the coast on either side (Gannon 2003:32). The new reservation was not as suitable for Native American horticulture and was smaller than the previous territory. As a result, the Indians were under severe pressure to feed their people. Although the American government provided some rations, cattle rustling became a frequent occurrence. In addition, the Seminole continued to harbor escaped slaves, a sore point with the planters. By 1832, the white settlers, anxious to acquire land in Central Florida, pushed for removal of the Seminole to the Indian territory of Oklahoma (Gannon 2003:32). Ultimately the conflict between whites seeking Indian lands and Indians seeking survival erupted in December 1835 as the Second Seminole War, a conflict that would last the next seven years and destroy the plantations of East Florida—this in spite of the fact that many of the East Florida planters maintained good relations with the Seminole and even hired them to work on their plantations (for example, at Bulow and Dummett).

Sugar production in East Florida reached its peak in the short 16-year period between the First and Second Seminole wars. During this period, most of the East Florida planters probably experimented with sugar; Griffin (1999:Table 1) identifies eight sugar producers in the Halifax and Mosquitoes area alone. Visitor Charles Vignoles, writing in 1823, said: "the accounts from East Florida, respecting the sugar cane, have been uncommonly favorable: several large establishments are about to be erected, and considerable investments are making for the express purpose of raising the cane. It is a matter of infinite satisfaction, that the certainty of sugar becoming the *staple* of Florida is already established" (Vignoles 1823:14; emphasis in original).

Florida continued to be influenced by the Caribbean sugar industry during this period. Recent research on the life of early-nineteenth-century settler Moses Elias Levy suggests that he may have been instrumental in the growth of sugar production during this period (Monaco 2005). Levy migrated to Florida from Cuba in May of 1822, "on a schooner that was laden with Cuban sugar cane, 'the first brought to the country,' according to the local inhabitants" (Monaco 2005:97). While this was certainly not the first sugar cane brought to Florida, Levy had a history as a merchant-shipper and planter in the Caribbean, and was determined to produce sugar on his newly acquired lands in Florida. While it is not clear how much influence Levy had on the planters in East Florida, particularly since his plantations were not that successful, his efforts do coincide with the appearance of major sugar plantations throughout the region. It should be remembered, however, that the modest success of sugar planters in coastal Georgia and South Carolina also influenced the Florida planters, some of whom came from that region.

Sugar continued to be a costly operation. Planters often took out large loans or mortgages to finance their operations. Joseph Hernandez mortgaged a half interest in his St. Joseph sugar plantation for $11,172.02 in 1834 and got a loan for $38,000 the following year (Cresap 1982:157). Thomas Dummett borrowed money both to purchase his plantation and to build his sugar works (Davidson 1950a), but still had trouble paying for its construction. Cruger and DePeyster in New Smyrna mortgaged their property for $5,000 in 1830 (Cresap 1982:157)—a note on which they defaulted. Based on these experiences of Hernandez (a major planter), Dummett, and Cruger and DePeyster, the properties were not producing sufficient sugar to cover the costs.

The Territorial Period remained a period of fierce competition in the sugar market, dominated by the Caribbean and Louisiana. By 1829, Cuba was producing more sugar than all of the combined British Caribbean colonies (Smith 2005:216). East Florida plantations also had to compete with sugar plantations in Central and Northwest Florida during this period. Speaking of those regions, historian Sidney Martin has said that "More cane was grown in the six years from 1829 to 1835 than in any other six years during the Territorial period. People in the vicinity of Tallahassee became highly enthusiastic over the increased production. Sugar became the money crop on three plantations in the Alachua section in 1833" (Martin 1944:114). Three of these plantations produced cane and molasses that averaged $300 per hand (slave), ranging from a low of $4,000 on the smallest plantation to $14,000 on the largest (Martin 1944:114).

East Florida's sugar plantations were such a minor factor in overall sugar production in the Americas that studies of sugar plantations in the region merely mention them in passing as small sugar-producing areas in North America (Galloway 1989; Mintz 1985; Smith 1973).

Statehood, 1835 to 1861

The Second Seminole War of 1835 to 1842 destroyed the sugar plantations of East Florida. Planters filed claims for damages, including a $40,000 claim for the John

Bulow sugar plantation (Cresap 1982:157). But settlement of these claims was slow and not certain; Bulow's was in fact refused. At the same time, "sugar prices collapsed in 1840–1870, making it impossible to sustain sugar production at a profitable level on marginal lands" (Barka 2001:138). Apparently the planters of East Florida weighed the low prices offered for sugar against the expenses of rebuilding, and opted to try other ventures. Only two of the properties described in this study were reestablished after the war (Dunlawton and Rees Spring Garden).

East Florida was no longer a factor in Florida sugar production. During the years before the Civil War, the major sugar-producing areas of Florida were Marion County, Northwest Florida, and the Manatee River area of Southwest Florida. In 1850, Marion County produced 508,000 pounds of sugar, and in 1860, Manatee County was second to Marion County in production (Cresap 1982:169). Planter Robert Gamble Jr. of Manatee County claimed in 1851 that "Our plantations will yield from 2000 to 3000 pounds of sugar to the acre. The cost of production will be from 1 to 1½ cents per pound" (qtd. in Smith 1973:68). In 1850, Gamble produced 230,000 pounds of sugar valued at $9,000. Fellow Manatee County planter John Braden produced 100,000 pounds that year, valued at $6,000 (Smith 1973:130–131).

Prior to the Civil War, Louisiana and Cuba dominated sugar production in the United States and the Caribbean. One scholar has written: "Although sugar cane was grown along the southeastern coast and near the Gulf Coast of Texas, the majority of sugar plantations [in the U.S.] were found in the so-called Sugar Bowl of southern Louisiana. By 1853 there were almost 1,300 of them, and collectively they accounted for one-fourth of the world's sugar production" (Sitterson 1953:45). In 1852, a single Louisiana plantation claimed production of $99,600 in sugar and syrup (Olcott 1857:123). During the same period, sugar production in Cuba increased to the point that 60 percent of the sugar used in the United States came from Cuba (Smith 2005:216).

Historian Sidney Martin sums up the economics of East Florida sugar production very well:

> Sugar cultivation had a bright future in Florida, but the keen competition with West Indian and Cuban sugar could not be withstood. There were other factors, too, which helped to reduce sugar production in Florida, including the lack of capital to grow effectively large quantities, the lack of experience on the part of the growers, and unskilled refiners. The [Second] Seminole War curtailed output also. All these things combined left Florida with nothing more than the hope that some day she might become a leading producer of sugar. Nevertheless the *St. Augustine News* [March 26, 1842] proclaimed that "the great staple of East Florida when the war is over must be sugar." (Martin 1944:114–115)

One can add to Martin's list: the competition from the massive Louisiana and Cuba plantations, which had an earlier start than Florida's and adapted more advanced technologies; a sometimes fitful climate that shortened the growing period; soil fertility problems; and low world sugar prices. There is also the separate issue of beet sugar, which spread across Europe in the early nineteenth century, further lowering the prices for cane sugar and reducing the market.

The Civil War effectively ended sugar production throughout Florida, except for small-scale production, primarily of molasses and cane syrup, for home use. Without the slave labor force, the economics of sugar production were not viable in Florida. It would not be until the Everglades drainage programs of the late nineteenth century, combined with the highly mechanized production of that period, that Florida would become a major sugar producer.

II
The Architecture of East Florida Sugar Plantations

The buildings, or to use a more planter like phrase, "a set of Sugar Works," must necessarily depend upon the means employed. Should a large capital be invested, then, and in that case, the works should be constructed of brick or stone, as the durability of the materials, would essentially add to the embellishment, security and value of the estate. If, however, the funds are inadequate to this end, those of wood may be established, which will prove fully as convenient and efficient, but not as durable.

—John C. Cleland, *The Superior Advantages to Be Derived from the Culture of Sugar-Cane, in East-Florida* (1836)

5
Architectural Influences

Any plantation reflected not only the local ecology and climate, but the consequences of a particular settlement history as well.
—John Michael Vlach, *Back of the Big House: The Architecture of Plantation Slavery* (1993)

What makes architecture important in understanding the history of an area? Historically so-called "high styles" of architecture become popular throughout the world during a particular period—for example, Gothic or Baroque architecture. But each culture and region adapt these styles in a way that reflects the environment and the historic events which occurred in the area, as well as the needs, beliefs, skills, and resources of the culture. By looking at the way buildings were constructed, used, modified, and reused, we can get insights into the people who produced them (Carter and Cromley 2005:xx).

Sugar Works as Vernacular Architecture

The sugar works of East Florida can be classified as industrial vernacular architecture. In the simplest sense, "vernacular architecture is the common building of a given place and time" (Mercer 1975:1). It is closely related to the community that produced it and tends to occur frequently within that community (Carter and Cromley 2005:8). While it is seldom designed or built by noted architects, vernacular architecture may reflect elements of popular styles of the period and region in which it is produced. In a sense, it is "the assembly of preexisting parts to solve a problem, make a tool, or otherwise create a physical solution" (Carter and Cromley 2005:15). Thus, when looking at the ruins of the sugar works, we need to consider the problem that was being solved—how to make sugar profitably—and how the particular structure attempted to solve that problem. We may be able to identify modifications that were made as the process changed, as well as the use of locally available materials. We may also be able to see influences from the dominant high styles of architecture during this period, which would primarily be the Federal, Georgian, and Classical Revival styles. All of these styles tend to emphasize symmetry, balance, and details that reflect the influence of features observed in Greek and Roman ruins.

Architectural Influences

By the time that the first serious attempts were made to produce sugar in Florida, during the British Period (1763 to 1783), Caribbean sugar plantations had been operating successfully for 150 years. These operations included a number of British colonies in the Caribbean. It was thus logical and natural that the new planters in Florida would import experts from the British Caribbean colonies to build and operate their sugar works. As historian Samuel Proctor said: "The colonies related especially to their borderlands—Georgia and the Carolinas to the north, Louisiana to the west, and the Caribbean to the south. The politics, the economics, the way of life in these areas affected the people of Florida—whites, blacks and Indians" (Proctor 1975:vii).

Public records from 1770 state that a Jamaican planter was employed at Richard Oswald's Swamp Settlement to make sugar and rum (in Payne and Griffin 2001:35). Another Jamaican planter, William Forbes, was employed by Andrew Turnbull at New Smyrna for the same purpose (Schafer 2008). This was a pattern that would be repeated in the Second Spanish Period (1783 to 1819). Several of the East Florida planters of the Second Spanish Period either came from the Caribbean or brought in experienced sugar makers from there. This included planters Robert McHardy from the Bahamas, Col. Thomas H. Dummett of Barbados, and John Bunch of Nassau. Dummett even hired a French sugar boiler, Monsieur Purseir, from the West Indies. Although little sugar was produced in the Bahamas, residents of those British islands would certainly have been familiar with sugar works on other British Caribbean islands such as Barbados, Jamaica, and Antigua. Given the planters' familiarity with the sugar works of the Caribbean, it is not surprising that the sugar works of East Florida are very similar to those of the Caribbean.

Another influence that should not be discounted is that of the early-nineteenth-century sugar planters of coastal Georgia and, to a lesser extent, South Carolina. Many of the settlers in Florida during the British, Second Spanish, and Territorial periods immigrated from the Carolinas and Georgia, where they may have been familiar with attempts to produce sugar in those regions. Charles and John Bulow of Bulowville, and Col. Orlando Rees of Spring Garden, for instance, were from South Carolina, as were several of the owners of Dunlawton. In addition, Thomas Spalding, a Georgia sugar planter, wrote extensively about not only sugar production but also the construction of masonry sugar works. His writings were published in the *Southern Agriculturist*, a popular journal for planters during the early nineteenth century (see Floyd 1937).

The Architecture

Beyond the obvious similarities in the sugar trains, mills, and distilleries, the Caribbean influence can be readily identified in the general layout of the buildings in the sugar works of East Florida. The plans of the earliest sugar works from the British Period (Oswald/Yonge's Three Chimneys and McHardy) are speculative at best, since most of the buildings were probably wood, and only the trains themselves remain. But once masonry construction was implemented, the similarities are immediately apparent.

A recent comparative analysis of sugar works in the Caribbean identified several different layouts: L-shaped, rectangular, rectangular with additions, square with an inner courtyard, T-shaped, T-shaped with additions, and separate buildings for each function (Meide 2003:26). Of these, the most common forms are L-shaped, T-shaped, and separate buildings. In the small sample set studied, the T shape was most common on British plantations (Meide 2003:26). A survey of sugar plantations in Tobago identified 43 sites, all dating to the post-1764 British Period. The survey found that "Site plans for the sugar factories are almost identical with the exception of the actual size of the buildings. Almost all of the factories are T shaped. A few factories were constructed differently in order to avoid topographic obstructions" (Eubanks 1992:110–111). The T and L are also the basic forms found in most of the sugar works of East Florida, as we will see in subsequent chapters. In contrast, the sugar works of French-influenced Creole Louisiana were very large rectangular buildings that concentrated all of the activities under a single roof (see, for example, Dunlawton in East Florida) (Vlach 1993:10–11).

Nineteenth-century writers provided specific recommendations as to the construction of sugar works. Henry Olcott (1857:112) showed an L-shaped building as the ideal shape (Figure 6). The short leg of the L contains a cane shed with the mill at the junction of the legs. The long leg has a boiling house separated by an open passage from the cooling house and purgery. The distillery is a separate building located between the legs of the L.

Planter Thomas Spalding of Georgia recommended that a sugar works "'should certainly be of brick, or tabby, as well to protect it against fire, as to preserve a warmth . . . to facilitate the running of your molasses'" (qtd. in Floyd 1937:97). Spalding advocated connecting the boiling room and curing room in an L or T configuration (Spalding 1816:243), much like those seen in many British Caribbean sites. Spalding specifically recommended many windows, and a latticed roof vent the length of the roof of the boiling house for ventilation and lighting, due to the volume of steam from sugar boiling. The curing house, on the other hand, needed to have few windows and preferably a flat roof to keep it warmer; stoves were also helpful to increase molasses draining (Spalding 1816:243).

Writing in East Florida in 1836, planter John Cleland recommended that the cooling shed should be located on the southeast end of the boiling house adjacent to the curing house (purgery). He further stated that both boiling house and curing house should "be in the same range and under the same shell, but each having a distinct roof, with a door or open communication" (Cleland 1836:24). If a still house is present, he recommended that it be conveniently located near the south end of the boiling house, and slightly lower to facilitate movement of molasses from the curing house cisterns (Cleland 1836:25). The bagasse storage building should be placed at least 50 yards from the boiling house to avoid the danger of fire. He recommended placing the crusher/mill on an elevation convenient to the cane fields, but where the juice would flow freely to the boiling house (Cleland 1836:27).

There was also a wide range of sizes in Caribbean sugar works, with English boiling houses falling into either the largest or smallest groups. Meide (2003:29) suggests that this may be because the English islands had both large and small planters engaged in sugar production. In general both the boiling house and the purgery tended to be rectangular. The purgeries were generally attached to the boiling house, most often in the T- or L-shaped configuration advocated by Spalding. Meide (2003:43) speculates that this was perceived as improving efficiency in terms of transferring the syrup to the purgery.

Perhaps even more important than nationality, however, were changes in technology. As the technology advanced, not only did the sugar works become more complex, they grew in size, both to encompass new technologies and also to handle the increased production that resulted from these improvements. The eighteenth-century British Period sugar works were little more than a sugar train with a sheltering roof. The animal-powered vertical mill was nearby and possibly open to the elements. The introduction of steam, and in one case in East Florida, water power, led to dramatic changes. The train went from four kettles with separate furnaces to the five-kettle Jamaica train with a single furnace. The mill itself became larger and required much more space for the engine, wheels, and belts. It also required shelter to protect the iron machinery from inclement weather. Greater production required a larger purgery. Masonry construction became the norm, perhaps for improved fire protection or to protect the more expensive equipment and valuable products.

The perception that sugar would be a profitable product led to an increased investment in the sugar works. Cleland (1836:40) estimated, perhaps unrealistically, that an acre of cane would yield 1,500 to 2,000 pounds of sugar which could sell for as much as 10 cents per pound. The correlation is obvious—the belief in a large crop of cane meant the need for the capacity to process that large crop efficiently and promptly.

The increased investment required for a masonry building and steam power in turn influenced the architecture. In 1816, Spalding (1816:236) recommended masonry for "the better appearance of the buildings"—obviously not a factor in production, but a matter of aesthetics. Buildings began to have finer details and more sophisticated construction such as arched windows and doors. Since the masonry of choice in East Florida was either coquina or tabby, a stuccoed exterior was a necessity to protect the porous masonry. As previously noted, tabby is a concrete made from lime from burnt shells, shells, sand, and water. It is relatively soft and porous; thus it was generally stuccoed. Coquina is a naturally occurring rock formed from small shells found along the coast of East Florida. As artist John James Audubon observed in 1831, "The fragments are cut out of the quarry with the common wood ax and fashioned with the same instrument for building" (qtd. in Strickland 1985:57). The stone hardens to an extent once exposed to the open air, but still benefits from a stucco coating. However, scoring the stucco to give the appearance of cut stone is a decorative touch which seems to say, "I am rich and powerful, so I can make even my industrial buildings attractive."

When we look at the sugar works ruins, we are looking for the specific spaces allotted for each step of the process: milling, clarification, boiling, curing, and storage. The individual spaces will vary depending on the level of technology as well as the extent of the planter's investment and experience. As previously noted, since this was a period of experimentation or adaptation to a certain extent, we will also see evidence of changes in the technology in some of the sugar works. There are four basic questions to ask of each sugar works (based on Carter and Cromley 2005:xvii): (1) is it a new idea or one that has been consistently used, (2) is it the only one of its kind in the community, (3) how does the layout compare to other sugar works, and (4) has it changed through time.

The following chapters will describe eight East Florida sugar works and tie the architectural features of each to the level of technology. The works will be compared to the others in the region to look for changes that reflect changes in the technology. The descriptions of the structures are primarily drawn from SouthArc's 2001 structural stabilization study (Wayne et al. 2001), supplemented by archaeological studies completed at several of the individual sites. All of the sites have been addressed in local histories, particularly Alice Strickland's *Ashes on the Wind* (1985), Edith Stanton's *Ruins of the Early Plantations of the Halifax Area, Volusia County, Florida* (1949), and H. Radford Bishop's "Plantations along the Halifax" (1975). In order to provide the individual site histories, these limited historic discussions have been supplemented by site-specific histories, primary records, and more recent archaeological and historic research completed by several scholars.

6
The Spanish Trains
Oswald/Yonge Three Chimneys and McHardy

That upon this settlement there was a large sugar house and every building
he believes necessary for a sugar plantation; they were built of very good
materials and good workmanship.
 —Robert Payne, "Deposition regarding Mount Oswald Plantation" (1786)

Two of the sugar works in the project area provide clear evidence of the earliest
and simplest form of sugar works—the four-kettle Spanish train. There were undoubtedly single-kettle operations on small properties, but this method would basically only generate syrup and possibly sugar for on-site consumption. Production
for the market required a more extensive operation. The Oswald/Yonge Swamp
Settlement property, dating from the British Period, has an intact Spanish train
and a small distillery. The sugar works remains on the McHardy plantation may
have been the same basic form in its earliest iteration—which also might date to
the British Period. The McHardy sugar works was later modified into a Jamaica
train, but evidence of its original Spanish train format can be readily seen. The oldest part of the Dunlawton sugar works may have been a Spanish train, but it was
later extensively modified into a four-kettle Jamaica train. This chapter will ad-
dress only the Oswald/Yonge site and McHardy.

Oswald/Yonge Three Chimneys

The Three Chimneys site, also known as Oswald's Swamp Settlement and the
Henry Yonge plantation, is located on the north side of S.R. 40 (West Granada
Boulevard) in Ormond Beach (Figure 1). It is now a state-owned historic park,
managed by the Ormond Beach Historical Society. Access to the site can be arranged via their Web page (www.ormondhistory.org) or at their visitors center at
38 East Granada Boulevard.

 Three Chimneys is one of only two of the sugar works in this study known to
have also produced rum (Dummett is the other). It is also believed to be the oldest
of the extant sugar works in this study and the only all-brick works in this book.
Reportedly there is another Spanish train dating to the British Period within the
Cape Canaveral National Seashore (Herschel E. Shepard Jr., architect, personal
communication 2009).

Richard Oswald's Swamp Settlement is the only sugar works remains in this study that can be definitely dated to the British Period. It is also the simplest form of sugar works. In essence, these sugar works would have consisted of an animal-powered vertical mill (see Figure 7), a four-kettle Spanish train (see Figure 10), a well, and—in the case of the Swamp Settlement—a small distillery. The train itself was probably sheltered by an open wooden structure much like the one shown in Figure 5, a seventeenth-century Caribbean sugar works.

Richard Oswald's efforts to establish a plantation in East Florida have been documented in several articles by historian Daniel Schafer (1982, 1999, 2000). The Three Chimneys site has also undergone several archaeological and architectural investigations, beginning in 1995 with excavations adjacent to the ruins by Ted Payne of MAAR Associates, Inc., and American Preservation Consultants, Inc. (Payne 1995). With input from Payne, experienced volunteers followed this testing with further excavation along the south side of the boiling house. In 1999, SouthArc, Inc., conducted a survey of the entire Three Chimneys tract and completed measured drawings of the ruins for a historic preservation plan for the site (Wayne et al. 1999). The site was revisited and reevaluated in 2001 by SouthArc for the structural stabilization plan that provides much of the architectural detail in this study (Wayne et al. 2001). The most recent archaeology at the site was again completed by Payne, who excavated part of the sugar train in 2007, and by the State Archaeologist's office, which completed additional testing and mapping for a National Register of Historic Places nomination (Payne 2007; Andrea White, archaeologist, personal communication 2008).

Oswald's Swamp Settlement History

The Swamp Settlement site first appeared as part of a grant to Juan Alonzo de Esquivel during the First Spanish Period (1565 to 1763). There is little evidence that any improvements were made on the tract during that period (Payne 1995:7).

Oswald Ownership. When the British acquired Florida in 1763, Governor James Grant realized that he needed settlers to replace the exodus of the Spaniards. With input from the East Florida Society of London, the governor devised a grant plan. The wealthy gentry in the society used their family connections and influence in Parliament to secure grants from the Privy Council (Schafer 1999:26). One of the society members was a Scotsman named Richard Oswald, a merchant, West Indies planter, slave trader, and friend of Governor Grant. Oswald presented his investment plan to Governor Grant in 1764, recommending acquisition of land on a navigable river, and installing approximately 20 "seasoned" slaves with an overseer. During the first year, the slaves would clear and fence approximately 100 acres, primarily for food and livestock; construct buildings; and purchase clothes and tools through sales of extra provisions. After that, additional slaves could be brought in from Africa (where Oswald coincidentally operated a slave-trading venture) (Schafer 1982:39–40).

Although the governor realized that developing plantations in Florida would be difficult, he went forward with Oswald's plan, seeking additional advice from longtime friends among the South Carolina planters. Several of these friends, including future Lieutenant Governor John Moultrie of South Carolina, also acquired large grants in Florida (Schafer 2000:13).

On July 20, 1764, Richard Oswald received a grant of 20,000 acres along the Halifax River (Barclay 1998:5). Although Oswald never visited his Florida property, he worked closely with his friend and silent partner, the governor, to immediately establish five settlements within the Mount Oswald grant. The governor helped select the lands for the grant—including areas previously cleared by Native Americans—and provided periodic supervision, while Oswald provided the money and labor, beginning with 30 slaves from South Carolina. Ultimately, Oswald had over 240 slaves on his Florida properties (Schafer 1999:26, 2000:15, 26). These settlements consisted of the main property, Mount Oswald; the Ferry Settlement on the Tomoka River; the Cowpens Settlement on the Tomoka River; the Swamp Settlement; and Adia south of Mount Oswald.

All did not go well with Oswald's plantations. His first overseer, Samuel Huey (or Hewie), was murdered by rebellious slaves in 1767. The governor replaced him with an Indian or mixed-race overseer named Johnson, who was better liked by the slaves (Barclay 1998:5; Schafer 1999:27). "Indian Johnson" left later the same year, and Oswald appointed Lt. John Fairlamb as his agent, with two overseers, Frederick Robinson and Donald McLean. Fairlamb left in 1772, and McLean left in 1773, leaving Robinson in charge (Schafer 1999:27).

The sugar works lies within the part of the grant known as the Swamp Settlement. This tract was developed in the late 1760s or early 1770s as a sugar plantation (Payne 1995:11; Schafer 1999:27). Public records indicate that Oswald brought an expert from Jamaica to plant his sugar cane and supervise construction of the sugar works, authorizing funding for a grinding mill, the kettles, and a distillery (Schafer 1999:28, 2000:24). He also provided cane seedlings from his Scottish hothouse (Schafer 2000:22). In 1773, an indentured carpenter at the Mount Oswald plantation, Malcolm Ross, wrote to Oswald that "it was expected that the Sugar Plantation will soon make up all the expenses your honour has been at" (Ross 1773). One visitor reported that the sugar cane "looks very good and he [Robinson] is building a sugar works" (Schafer 1999:28). But in 1774, planter John Moultrie stated that "At Oswald's the man [James] Brown that he sent out has been making a mill to grind cane for 2 years past. Tis just finished since the cane was destroyed [by an early frost]" (Schafer 1999:28). A year later, however, another planter, Frederick George Mulcaster, stated that "The sugar plantation at the Mount goes on also" (Schafer 1999:28).

Although Oswald may have successfully produced both rum and sugar at the Swamp Settlement, it apparently was not at a profitable level. In the late British Period, both the American Revolution and stiff competition from the West Indies plantations impacted his plantations (Strickland 1976:3). By 1786, Lt. Col. John Douglas described the plantation as abandoned and in a state of decay, although he believed the buildings had been in use only three or four years earlier (Siebert 1972:60). In actuality, based on a report from Robert Payne, Oswald abandoned the property in 1781 or 1782 (Payne 1786). Oswald moved his slaves and everything portable to his Georgia landholdings (Schafer 1999:28; Butts 1967:2). One report stated that Mount Oswald's settlements were vacated in 1780 because of possible attack by Spanish privateers. When Savannah was occupied by the Americans, Oswald returned his slaves to Florida in 1782, although activity was limited to the main settlement of Mount Oswald and the Swamp Settlement (Siebert 1972:58; Schafer 1999:29; Butts 1967:2). This may indicate that sugar was still considered a potentially profitable product by Oswald and Grant. Oswald abandoned all of his grant when the Spanish reacquired Florida in 1783.

When Oswald's widow filed a claim for losses due to the Treaty of Paris, which turned Florida over to Spain, three descriptions were provided in support of her claims:

1. Robert Payne, who visited in 1781 or 1782, described 100 acres cleared for sugar. But since this had not been successful, the effort had been abandoned. He also described a large sugar house and other buildings, which were well constructed and in good condition when he visited, but since abandoned (Payne 1786).
2. Lieutenant Governor John Moultrie described 200 or 300 cleared acres used for provisions, indigo, and sugar. He also stated that there were buildings for a sugar works, but he didn't know their condition since he had last visited in 1779 (Moultrie 1786).
3. Lt. Col. John Douglas also said there were 300 cleared acres, partly back swamp and partly oak hammock. The swamp was used for sugar. He felt that the buildings could be repaired for £100. However, he felt that the plan-tation was too far north for sugar and would be better used for indigo. He further stated that 200 acres had been used for indigo and provisions. He listed a frame one-story overseer's house, slave cabins, a sugar house that could be converted to a barn, a corn house, and cowpens. He recommended that the utensils for the sugar plantation be used to boil indigo (Douglas 1786:60–61).

The sugar house that Douglas indicated could be converted to a barn was prob-ably either the purgery, the fermentory, or a storage building for filled barrels.

His comment that the sugar works could be used for boiling indigo suggests that Douglas was not familiar with indigo processing, which does not involve boiling; rather it uses large tanks for soaking the plants (Taylor 1984:41). The descriptions in the claims are the only information we have on the overseer's house and slave cabins; clearly they were modest wood-framed structures.

Although Mary Oswald filed a claim for £9,298 10s., the final settlement was only £3,921 5s. (Siebert 1972:330). It is, of course, possible that Oswald's agent inflated the value of the improvements on the property in order to increase the total claim amount. Thus the final settlement may be more realistic in terms of actual values.

Yonge Ownership. In 1803, during the Second Spanish Period (1783 to 1819), 850 acres of the Mount Oswald grant, encompassing the former Swamp Settlement, were granted to 19-year-old Don Enrique (Henry) Yonge. Henry Yonge was a Georgia-born resident of the Bahamas (Strickland 1985:34). As a resident of the Bahamas, Yonge may have been familiar with sugar cultivation and production in the Caribbean. He acquired a severely deteriorated settlement with only six slaves and limited funds to improve the property (Strickland 1985:34). Although the abandoned Swamp Settlement sugar works was located in Yonge's grant, it probably was in poor condition after 20 years of disuse. Yonge's shortage of funds led him to sell one of his slaves, but after only six years, he abandoned the property and moved to Georgia (Strickland 1985:34).

Post-Sugar Ownership. Between Yonge's abandonment of the property in 1809 and 1850, the Swamp Settlement changed hands a number of times, although there is little indication that any substantial activity occurred within the tract. Certainly it was not again used for sugar after its abandonment by Yonge.

Anna Maria Hill acquired the 850-acre property in 1811, but it was sold to Octavius Mitchal in 1820. Mitchal in turn sold it to John (Don Juan) McQueen in 1822. After certifying and mapping the property, McQueen sold it to John P. Williamson in 1823; Williamson's title was confirmed in 1845. In 1850 it was acquired by William, Rudolphus, and Obed Swift (operating as the Swift Brothers) for logging of live oak (Payne 1995:21). The Swifts retained ownership until 1874, when the property again changed hands several times until it was acquired in 1875 by Philip and Francina Corbin (Hinkley 1931:31).

The Corbins developed a new community on the former Yonge grant, which they named New Britain. This would evolve into present-day Ormond Beach (Strickland 1985:34). By 1914, William Fagan (or Fagen) was living on the tract containing the sugar works ruins. He legally acquired this property in 1916 and built a house that incorporated the ruins of the sugar train (Figure 16). Fagan operated a tourist attraction on the property until he sold it to Edmund L. Fisher in 1921 (Payne 1995:21).

16. Fagan House at Oswald/Yonge Three Chimneys. (Courtesy of the Halifax Historical Museum, Daytona Beach, Florida)

Between Fagan's sale of the property in 1921 and the 1940s, the tract was apparently a picturesque ruin (Anderson and Price ca. 1890:24). Sometime prior to 1948, it was acquired by William H. Flegert, who operated a small farm on the property until it was sold to Sun Beach Investment Company in 1994 (Payne 1995:21). In 2001, the property surrounding the sugar works ruins was acquired by the State of Florida, and it is now managed by the Ormond Beach Historical Society.

Oswald/Yonge Three Chimneys Sugar Works

Although the 1786 depositions indicate that the Swamp Settlement contained a large sugar house, as well as other buildings, since the structures were primarily wood, little remains today other than the Fagan chimney, the boiling train (Figure 17), and the small distillery furnaces. The train has recently been stabilized, but the distillery is seriously deteriorated, and its chimney has collapsed. The sugar train does provide a good understanding of how a Spanish train looked and operated. There is no evidence of the mill for grinding the cane. Logic says it was probably located near the sugar train, and most likely closest to the east (*grande*) end where the sugar process begins. It was almost certainly a vertical animal-powered

17. South side of Oswald/Yonge Three Chimneys sugar train.

mill. Nor is there evidence of the curing shed, which was probably a simple wood building long since deteriorated. Payne (1996a:4) did find hand-wrought nails around the train and to the east, supporting the presence of frame structures.

The site is known as Three Chimneys, but the only eighteenth-century chimney still existing is that for the distillery; the Spanish train would not have had a chimney. It is possible that the other two chimneys that gave the site its nickname were for the overseer's house or slave cabins, although locations of these structures remain unknown. There are older references to the site as simply "the Chimney" (Fenty 1976) or "Old Chimneys" (Taylor ca. 1980), which may more realistically reflect what existed at the site.

Since the Swamp Settlement dates to the initial settlement of this area in the mid-eighteenth century, its sugar works has a simple four-kettle Spanish train. As previously noted, it may have been very similar in layout and appearance to the complex shown in a seventeenth-century drawing from the Caribbean (Figure 5), although the sugar train itself may have been enclosed in the building described in the depositions. The descriptions below are based primarily on documentation completed by SouthArc, Inc. (Wayne et al. 1999, 2001).

The Sugar Train. The sugar train was constructed of brick in a trapezoidal shape to accommodate the decreasing sizes of the kettles (Figure 18). Each firebox is slightly smaller as the train progresses from east to west—corresponding with the kettles that once rested in the train. One oddity is present: a large, flat area on the

THREE CHIMNEYS, 8Vo196
ORMOND BEACH, FLORIDA

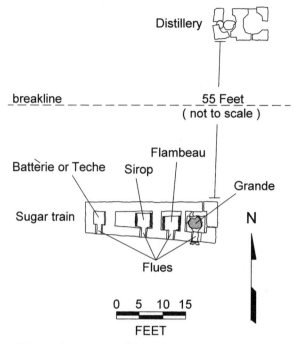

18. Plan of Oswald/Yonge Three Chimneys sugar works.

west side of the firebox for the *sirop*, the next-to-last kettle going west (Figures 18 and 19). Archaeologist Ted Payne (2007:19) has suggested that this was where the clarifier sat, but that would be inconsistent with the normal operation of a sugar train, in which the clarifier would have preceded the *grande*. An experienced rum maker suggested that it could have been a resting place for lime water added to the sugar solution (Ceylon Barclay, personal communication 1999). Alternatively, it could have simply been a resting place for tools or buckets used in stirring and transferring the syrup.

The brick in the train is English cross or common bond with alternating rows of headers and stretchers (McKee 1973:78), resulting in approximately two-foot-thick outer walls. It rests on a foundation of a double course of brick laid flat on a sand bed with no footing. The brick is almost all hand formed, slightly smaller than modern brick. The bricks are lightweight but very dense. Noticeable surface striations and warping suggest they were fired at high heat. By modern standards, these bricks would be classified as "clinkers," or waste bricks, but the skillful masons who

19. Looking east at Oswald/Yonge Three Chimneys sugar train.

built the train took advantage of the warping to form the contours of the firing chambers, facilitating a better interface between the bricks and the metal kettles. Voids between the warped bricks were filled with mortar.

The north side of the train clearly shows the series of rebuilding that this sugar works underwent (Figure 20). The lower bricks, at the level of a series of recessed openings, run approximately two-thirds of the length of that side. These bricks are the same dark red/brown clinker brick found on the other three sides of the structure. The upper brick and the entire west end of this side are built of light-colored bricks—possibly due to a lime wash over the surface. Otherwise, these bricks are identical in size and form to those in the balance of the train. This suggests that part of the north side was reconstructed, possibly by Henry Yonge, using bricks salvaged from another structure. Finally, there are areas of modern machine-made brick along the top of the north wall. These bricks match those of the nearby Fagan chimney. Based on photographs and descriptions of Fagan's house (Figure 16), this brick formed the support for the south side of his house where it rested on the old sugar train.

The mortar in the original Oswald/Yonge train is a light grayish brown composed of coarse sand with small shell inclusions; this is the type of mortar known in the coastal Southeast as tabby mortar. It is fairly consistent throughout, and was

20. North side of Oswald/Yonge Three Chimneys sugar train.

tooled flush with the brick faces. The mortar joints are wider than is customary, probably to accommodate the misshapen bricks.

The north side of the train was the side on which the workers stood. Nine regularly spaced pockets located on this side (Figure 20) probably supported the ends of joists for a platform along this side of the train (cf. Figure 10). There is no pocket at the east end, but archaeological testing (Payne 1995:Figure 14) indicated a layer of brick at ground level at this corner. This suggests that the platform ended short of the corner with a step down to ground level.

The south side of the train has four furnace openings (Figure 17). The easternmost opening retains a two-part cast-iron flue; the upper part is an inverted U shape resting on the lower flat plate (Figure 21). Both pieces are approximately two inches thick and extend approximately two feet into the chamber. Again, curved clinker brick was used to conform to the shape of the flue in the wall above the liner. The brick construction and rust remains in the other fireboxes indicate that they had similar iron flues, but at different heights in order to manage the different levels of heat required for each kettle.

As is standard in a Spanish train, each firebox is self-contained with no openings between them (Figures 18 and 22). Air would have been drawn through the single flue and smoke emitted through the firebox openings and possibly around

21. Reconstructed flue under *grande* kettle, Oswald/Yonge Three Chimneys.

22. Looking west at Oswald/Yonge Three Chimneys sugar train.

the kettles. Small ledges found in each firebox with semicircular depressions in the mortar and rust fragments indicate that iron bars or grating separated the fireboxes into two levels, with the fire on the grating and ash in the bottom. Fuel was introduced through the flue liners onto the grate. Based on this construction and the variation in levels, it appears that the heat was controlled not by the size of the fire or firebox, but by proximity to the kettles.

Although the upper portions of the sugar train are missing, similar trains would have had either a vaulted top or contoured top to insure that spillage drained back to the *flambeau*. Tabby concrete was available at the time of construction of the train, and could have been used to cap the brick structure and form such a cover. The plastic nature of the tabby would have been ideal for interfacing with the metal kettles. Slight remnants of brick arching in some of the dividing walls between the chambers suggest that a vaulted top was present.

The Distillery. The ruins of the small distillery are built of brick and coquina (Figures 23 and 24). The structure has two side-by-side fireboxes on an east-west axis (Figure 18). This double configuration would correspond to a pot still, or doubler still (Payne 1995:18) (see Figure 15). The collapsed chimney apparently served both fireboxes.

The distillery was constructed of coquina blocks placed on grade. The 1995 archaeological study indicated that there is mortared brick rubble below the coquina (Payne 1995:55). The rectangular coquina blocks are placed around the perimeter of the structure. Inside the fireboxes, brick is dry-laid flat on a sand bed with a wash of lime over the brick surface. A second course of coquina blocks is found at each of the corners above the foundation course. These corner blocks serve to lock together the adjacent sides. Burnt clay brick, similar to that in the sugar train, is installed in an English cross bond pattern above the coquina. The tabby mortar matches that of the sugar train: lime-based tabby with coarse sand and shell inclusions.

A small ledge is built into the interior of each firebox. Based on the similar size and location of these ledges to those in the sugar train, they probably held a grating to separate the fireboxes into upper and lower levels. The area below the ledge is rectangular, while the upper area is circular to fit the cylindrical distillery vessels. Like the sugar train, the upper area used the misshapen bricks to create a contour to receive the cylindrical still vessels. The upper portion of all of the walls has been disturbed, so it cannot be determined how they were capped or how the tops of the fireboxes were configured.

There are openings for the fireboxes on the north side. At the time of the Payne (1995:50) survey, one brick in the west box suggested a low arched opening. The remnants of iron strap hinges are found on the west jamb of the east firebox. Rust discoloration on the brick of the east jamb suggests the location of missing hardware for a cast-iron door.

23. North side of distillery, Oswald/Yonge sugar works.

24. South side of distillery, Oswald/Yonge sugar works.

25. Distillery at Three Chimneys, ca. 1910. (Courtesy of the Florida Memory Project, Florida State Archives, Tallahassee, Florida)

The brick chimney was still standing in 1995; it was recorded as 12.6 feet high, flush with the north wall of the distillery (Payne 1995:50). When standing, the chimney was located between the two fireboxes, aligned with the north wall (Figure 25). The south face of the chimney widened at the bottom to provide stability, and created flues for the fireboxes on either side. Based on old photographs, the chimney tapered at the top (Figure 25).

Several components of the rum-making process are missing at the site: the distillery vessels and coils, the water tank for cooling the coils, and a protective roof or building. It is probable that these elements were salvaged for reuse elsewhere or, in the case of wood, simply decayed. Fragments of iron pipe coils were found in the rubble of the east firebox in 1995 (Payne 1995:55).

A well and a modern well house are located approximately 40 feet north of the distillery. While the extant well dates to 1954, according to a date incised in the concrete (Wayne et al. 1999:72), it may cover a historic well, based on the circular concrete trough around the well pipe. There certainly would have been a well located somewhere around the sugar works, since abundant water is necessary for both sugar boiling and rum making.

Oswald/Yonge Three Chimneys Summary. The sugar works at the Swamp Settlement is important for several reasons. It contains one of two extant distillery remains in the study area; the other is at Dummett. It illustrates sharing of building typologies and technologies between the settlements in East Florida and those of the British Caribbean. It blends indigenous materials (coquina and tabby mortar) with imported building techniques and methods. And, it contributes to our understanding of construction techniques in the region.

The McHardy Site

The McHardy site is located in an undeveloped area of Tomoka State Park between the Old Dixie Highway and the Tomoka River (Figure 1). It is presently not accessible to visitors due to its remote location. The site consists of two components: (1) a house site with the remains of three structures and a well, and (2) the separate sugar works located approximately 1½ miles to the east. The sugar works may not be related to the house site and may, in fact, predate it.

Although the McHardy house site has had limited archaeological investigations, very little has been done at the sugar works. Archaeologist John W. Griffin tested the house site in the early 1950s and completed drawings of the remains (Patricia C. Griffin, anthropologist, personal communication 2001). When the Halifax Plantation Development was planned, state archaeologists conducted a reconnaissance survey which included this site. They completed field drawings of the house site and sugar works remains as part of the survey (Daniel et al. 1980). Several years later, Jay Bushnell and his students from Daytona Beach Community College cleared the remains of the smaller structure at the house site, documenting a tabby floor (Jay Bushnell, retired professor, personal communication 2001). The most recent work involved additional testing of the house site by archaeologist Ted Payne (Payne 1996b). The 2001 stabilization study by SouthArc included probing and updating the measured drawings of the sugar works ruins (Wayne et al. 2001).

History of McHardy

The area of the McHardy site first appears as a grant to James Moncrief during the British Period (1763–1783). Moncrief received a 1,000-acre parcel where he established a settlement called Damietta, and began cultivation. The last record of his cultivation is in 1777, and he abandoned the property in 1778 (Payne 1996b:5).

McHardy Ownership. During the Second Spanish Period, in 1808, Robert McHardy acquired a 1,000-acre tract in the Mosquitos (Halifax River) area. McHardy was a Scotsman who was familiar with the properties in the area due to his position as surveyor of the land grants in East Florida, as well as through his father-in-law, Tomoka River planter John Bunch (Daniel et al. 1980:107; Payne 1996b:5; Patricia C. Griffin, anthropologist, personal communication 2001). McHardy married Mary Dean Bunch in 1798 in the Bahamas. After he lost most of his money in an 1802 investment, the couple left Nassau and moved to Spanish East Florida, where John Bunch provided them with nine slaves. Mary Dean Bunch McHardy was then able to petition for a land grant based on the headrights assignable to her family and her ownership of slaves (Strickland 1966:1; Payne and Griffin 2001:46).

The grant to land in the Mosquitos area was issued to Robert McHardy in 1808, although his wife was actually the owner. She had died the previous year, but the grant process was already under way at the time of her death. She willed her landholdings to her six-year-old son, John B. B. McHardy. After her death, the child was sent back to Nassau to his uncle, William B. Nunnings, the governor of the Bahamas. Robert McHardy supervised the family operations from then until his own death in 1822 (Strickland 1966:1; Payne and Griffin 2001:46).

There is some confusion in the records as to the size and exact location of McHardy's property. The McHardys may have been living on property adjoining John Bunch's, although they did not own it prior to 1815. After the Mosquitos grant was confirmed in 1815, McHardy exchanged that property for the 1,000-acre Tomoka tract, which was then listed in his name, rather than that of his son, the rightful owner (WPA 1941:102; Payne and Griffin 2001:46). The Tomoka grant is variously described as 1,000 acres, 745.42 acres, and 1,762 acres (Payne 1996b:5). Presumably it included all or part of the Moncrief Damietta tract; it immediately abutted John Bunch's plantation to the south. McHardy lived on the plantation until his second marriage to Carolina Williams in 1816, when he began living at least part time in New Smyrna at his new wife's plantation (Strickland 1966:2).

McHardy and his second wife both died in 1822, and the property was listed for sale soon afterward (Strickland 1966:2). An 1823 advertisement in the *East Florida Herald* for the sale of McHardy's plantation notes: "The buildings on the plantation are very commodious. There is a convenient new dwelling house, erected about two years ago, and only required a little inside work to be completed. Another dwelling house which was occupied by the late proprietor, a number of out houses such as a large cotton house, a gin house, kitchen and other outbuildings, a sufficient number of negro houses for fifty slaves" (qtd. in Strickland 1985:27). Note that there is no mention of a sugar works in this detailed description of the property. Nor did the ad mention cultivation of sugar, although it did say that some of the land, if cleared, would be suitable for cane (Strickland 1985:27). This leads to the possibility that the original sugar works may date to the earlier Moncrief ownership and was not used by McHardy at all.

McHardy's partially completed house was a modest structure approximately 35 by 40 feet with chimneys at either end. It was probably frame on a coquina-block foundation. The foundation suggests three rooms, although there may have been interior partitions. There was a separate kitchen building, a well, and a possible slave cabin nearby (Payne 1996b:11, 14).

Post-McHardy Ownership. At the time of the Second Seminole War 15 years

later, the plantation was owned by the Marquis de Fougeres, former French con-
sul in Charleston, South Carolina. Like the other properties in the area, it was destroyed at the beginning of the war (Strickland 1985:29).

By the late nineteenth century, this property was part of extensive acreage
owned by Norman Harwood. Harwood operated a cattle ranch and attempted to
develop a small community platted as Harwood. In 1915, the Harwood Land Company sold the acreage to another would-be developer, Conrad-Oates Company.
This development also failed, and the then-4,000 acres were subdivided among
several citrus growers. In the 1940s, cattleman E. B. Smoak acquired both Moncrief's original Damietta grant and the neighboring John Moultrie Rosetta plantation (Daniel et al. 1980:113). Smoak ultimately sold the property to developers and
the state. As previously noted, both the McHardy house site and the possibly earlier sugar works are now part of Tomoka State Park.

The McHardy Sugar Works

The McHardy sugar works appears to be a Spanish train that was modified into
the later Jamaica format. This sugar works is in a very deteriorated state, which
makes it difficult to fully delineate the site features (Figure 26). This description is
based on the 2001 evaluation of the site (Wayne et al. 2001).

The most visible features are a well and an adjacent sugar train (Figure 26). A
large rubble pile extending northeast from the sugar train is from the collapsed
chimney (Figure 27). Coquina wall foundations perhaps 18 inches wide extend
from the west side of the train for approximately 20 feet, delineating the outer
walls of the sugar works (Figure 27). This suggests that the sugar works was a wood
frame structure resting on a coquina foundation. Based on the size of the enclosed
area, it encompassed the cooling area and well. The purgery and mill locations remain unknown, although both were probably nearby. A newspaper article dating to
Smoak's ownership of the property described finding "A circular structure, 18 feet
in diameter, with walls three to four feet thick" near the train (Davidson ca. 1950).
While the article speculated that this was the purgery, it is more likely that it was
related to a vertical mill.

The train itself had four kettles like the Three Chimneys train, each originally
built with a separate firebox on the east side (Figure 27). The presence of a chimney at the southeast corner (Figure 27) argues that there is now a continuous flue
between the kettles; this could not be confirmed due to the collapsed masonry of
the kettles.

The exterior walls are well-dressed coquina blocks, while the interior seems to
be primarily constructed of rubble. The coquina in the train was shaped to fit the
kettles. There are a few well-made hand-molded bricks in the kettle areas, some

26. Southeast side of McHardy sugar train and well.

of which have been modified, probably to hold the kettles. The mortar joints in the structure are tooled, and the structure does not appear to have been plastered. Fragments of melted lead are present in the train, presumably part of the construction.

The chimney is offset from the train and has a cold (not interlocked) joint between chimney and sugar train (Figure 28). This further supports the theory that it represents a later modification. There are also differences in the mortars; the train is built with tabby mortar containing identifiable oyster fragments, while the chimney has sand mortar (Ted M. Payne, archaeologist, personal communication 2001). The chimney was built of large dressed coquina blocks with a brick lining.

Firebricks in the chimney flue, in the lower portion of the chimney fall, and scattered around the ruins are marked "Berry's Premium Firebrick" (Figure 29). Some of these bricks, like those in the kettles, have been modified to fit the flue, resulting in partial lettering. Identical marked bricks were noted at the nearby Dummett sugar works and at the McIntosh sugar works in Camden County, Georgia (Eubanks 1985:80). The origin and date range of these bricks could not be conclusively determined, although archaeologist James A. Ford identified the McIntosh bricks as having been made by William Berry of Georgia after 1819 (Ford 1937:221). Both Dummett and the McIntosh sugar works date to the mid-1820s, so it is plausible that they got their bricks from William Berry's brickworks. This

McHARDY PLANTATION, 8Vo244
TOMOKA BASIN GEOPARK

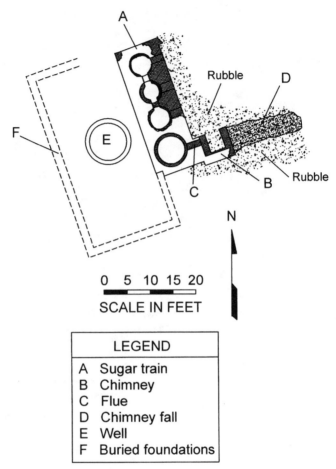

27. Plan of McHardy sugar works.

further supports the argument that the McHardy works were modified sometime after McHardy's period of ownership (1808 to 1822) from an eighteenth-century Spanish train to the Jamaica train more common in the nineteenth century.

The close proximity of the well to the west edge of the sugar train (slightly over three feet) indicates that the working platform, which would have been on that side of the train was quite narrow. The wall of the train on this side was stepped out approximately 1.5 feet, probably as a support for the workers' platform (Figure 26). The well itself is dressed coquina blocks.

28. Detail of McHardy sugar train chimney.

29. Berry's Premium Firebrick, McHardy sugar works.

Due to the thickly wooded area surrounding the McHardy sugar works, and the limited archaeological testing that has been conducted, there is presently no information on any associated features, such as the mill or circular foundation, at this site. There is also no evidence for a distillery. Given the lack of evidence for a steam engine at McHardy, the mill would probably have been the vertical animal-powered type typical of the eighteenth- to early-nineteenth-century sugar works (see Figure 7).

Summary of Spanish Train Sugar Works

Based on the remains of the Oswald/Yonge Three Chimneys and McHardy sugar works, it appears that British Period sugar works consisted of simple Spanish trains in wood frame structures, probably with vertical animal-powered mills. Although the Oswald/Yonge site is brick, both sites have evidence of the use of native materials—coquina block, tabby, and tabby mortar—in construction of sugar works that followed Caribbean models. In fact, there is confirmation that the Oswald/Yonge site was built by a Jamaican. It is equally likely that the McHardy sugar works was built by someone from the Caribbean, or at least someone familiar with the Caribbean sugar works. The later modifications to McHardy may have their origins in either the Caribbean or nearby southeast Georgia.

The simple form of these sugar works may be related to the fact that Florida during the British Period was very much a frontier; the British were basically the first settlers of this region. They may have been reluctant to invest substantial funds and manpower in construction of large sugar works until they determined that sugar would be a successful product in Florida.

7
The Adaptive Sugar Works
Dummett and Spring Garden

The source of power for the mills has to be reliable; otherwise planters
risked the spoilage of their crop.
—J. H. Galloway, "Tradition and Innovation in the
American Sugar Industry, c. 1500–1800" (1985)

We have already seen at the McHardy sugar works how technological advances
were adopted by planters—sometimes by reworking existing facilities. Galloway
(1985:335) reasonably argues that "planters adopted innovations only when it made
good economic sense to do so." Clearly the single-furnace Jamaica train was more
efficient to operate than the four furnaces required for a Spanish train. The use of
a chimney with the continuous flue may also have provided more consistent heat
under the kettles. The fire in the Jamaica train is at the far end of the train from the
chimney. The fact that the heat level dropped with distance from the fire may have
made control of the boiling process easier than separate fires under each kettle.

Based on the firebricks present in the chimney at McHardy, it seems to have
been altered in the mid-1820s. Interestingly, the Jamaica train was widespread in the
Caribbean, including the British colonies, by 1725 (Galloway 1985:342). Therefore
it is somewhat of a puzzle why those familiar with sugar making in the Caribbean
would have built Spanish trains during the British Period in East Florida. The answer may lie in the scale of the operations at the plantations of that period. Based
on Galloway's argument that economics drives innovation, if production was not
great, the investment required for construction of the more complex Jamaica train
as well as the skills to operate it may not have been considered worthwhile.

Another area of experimentation and innovation in sugar processing was in the
power used to drive the mills. Initially, mills were animal powered, but this is not
the most efficient system for grinding the cane for several reasons. First, the speed
fluctuated, which caused uneven wear on the rollers. Second, the teams of animals
had to be changed periodically, resulting in a stoppage in the grinding process.
Speed and time are critical to extraction of high-quality juice from cane. Third,
a large number of animals would be needed in order to provide teams around the
clock. Fourth, animal-powered mills required more slaves to tend the cattle and
operate the mill. One estimate stated that 18 slaves would be required for a cattle
mill or windmill, while a steam mill required only 5 (Satchell 2002:246). In summary, animal-powered mills were both inefficient and expensive.

Experiments with other power sources came as early as the seventeenth century in the Caribbean, where both wind- and water-powered mills were implemented in an environment conducive to those systems. The windmill required a dependable, constant breeze—a situation that was largely confined to the easternmost Caribbean islands (Galloway 1985:345). A water-powered mill required a source of water with sufficient head power to run the mill (Figure 30). This was a more limited situation in much of the Caribbean and in the sugar areas of the South, although by the 1830s Thomas Spalding of Georgia was operating a water-powered mill. He had excavated a five-acre pond, one foot deep, on his plantation to provide a one-foot head of water at high tide for his water-powered mill. This tidal flow produced 10 horsepower for six hours twice a day—enough to operate a horizontal roller mill (Sitterson 1953:138). During the period when steam engines were being introduced to the sugar industry, "water power, where accessible, was still more economical than steam" (Ward 1988:101).

The major development in power for mills was the steam engine. Experiments were made as early as 1768 in Jamaica to adopt the Newcomen steam engine to power sugar mills, and by 1810 steam power was present throughout the British colonies (Satchell 1997:1). For example, between 1803 and 1830, 132 Boulton and Watt engines were shipped to the sugar plantations in the New World—including plantations in Louisiana (Satchell 1997:1). Not only did the steam engine remove the need for a stock of cattle, it also provided a reliable, constant source of energy. As Cynric R. Williams wrote in his *Tour through the Island of Jamaica in the Year 1823*, "besides saving the planters' oxen and mules [a steam engine] enabled him to grind his canes and finish his crop with much greater expedition than with the old and usual medium of the cattle mill" (qtd. in Satchell 1997:11). The energy provided by the steam engine supported the change to more powerful horizontal iron mills, particularly after the introduction of the high-pressure engine after 1820.

The downside to steam engines was the need to have a skilled operator not only to set up the engine, but to run it and maintain it. Boulton and Watt solved this problem by offering training at their factory in England (Satchell 1997:4). According to an 1812 memo from James Watt, trained mechanics were in high demand and could require round-trip passage to and from England, board and lodging, medical expenses, a salary of £150 to £200 starting when a contract is signed, and the right to install engines for other planters (with a suitable salary adjustment) (in Satchell 1997:4–5). On top of all these requirements, the recruit's expenses had to be paid while he was in training (Satchell 1997:5). Parts were also a constant expense with steam engines (Satchell 1997:3).

Two of the sites in East Florida provide evidence of adaptation of new sources of power for their milling operations. The Dummett sugar works was possibly the first steam-powered mill in the area, and Spring Garden at DeLeon Springs is the only water-powered mill known in East Florida.

30. Sugar works in Surinam, by Pierre Jacques Benoit, 1839. (Courtesy of the John Carter Brown Library at Brown University)

Dummett Plantation

The Dummett sugar works is located on the east side of Old Dixie Highway two miles north of the Tomoka State Park entrance (Figure 1). Park information can be found at www.floridastateparks.org/tomoka. Limited roadside parking is available, and the park is open from 8 a.m. to sunset, although the Dummett ruins are fenced. The site consists of the remains of the coquina sugar works and two wells, one on the interior of the structure and one on the exterior.

The Dummett site was examined and documented with both plan and profile drawings in the early 1950s by archaeologist John W. Griffin (1952a). Limited archaeological testing has been completed at the site by Ted Payne of American Preservation Consultants, Inc., primarily in search of the slave cabins (Payne 1999). The 2001 stabilization study completed by SouthArc, Inc., included measured drawings of the ruins (Wayne et al. 2001).

History of Dummett

The Dummett property was originally part of the Rosetta plantation of the lieutenant governor of East Florida, John Moultrie. Moultrie was a former South Carolina planter and friend of Governor Grant. He received two adjoining 1,000-acre grants in East Florida, which he named Rosetta. Moultrie installed a manager at his Rosetta property in 1767. The plantation primarily produced rice and indigo, but corn, sugar cane, and provisions were also grown. By 1777, the main house, outbuildings, barns, and slave housing had been completed; no sugar works are mentioned in the records. William Forbes, a sugar planter from Jamaica hired by Andrew Turnbull for his ill-fated New Smyrna colony, visited Moultrie's plantation in 1770. He noted cane being grown there and volunteered to make sugar for Moultrie, but reported that there was no mill. He managed to improvise a sugar works out of iron kettles and small rollers, producing 22 pounds of sugar from 43 gallons of juice. This successful production encouraged him to support cane production at New Smyrna (Forbes 1770).

Bunch-Dummett Ownership. When the British ceded Florida back to Spain in 1783, Moultrie abandoned Rosetta, and it was granted to John Bunch in 1804. Bunch occupied the property for approximately 20 years, at which time he sold 2,175 acres, with about 90 slaves, to Thomas H. Dummett for $13,000 (Strickland 1985:23; Schene 1976:31–32). Dummett paid $2,000 down and obtained a mortgage from James and Charles Lawton for the balance; he also borrowed money from the Lawtons to establish a sugar works (Davidson 1950a).

Dummett was a former British Marine officer who had been a sugar planter in Barbados until an uprising in 1816 (Schene 1976:31–32). He lived briefly in Connecticut but moved to Florida in search of a warmer climate (Payne and Griffin 2001:58). Dummett's daughter, Anna, left a description of the plantation, and there is also an earlier map of the Bunch property which sheds some light on other buildings within the plantation. Anna Dummett (1949:9) described the main house as a log building with a palmetto thatched roof and a fireplace with brass andirons. Although a simple structure, it was apparently well furnished, perhaps with furnishings purchased from Bunch (Dummett 1949:9; Payne and Griffin 2001:58). Although an article in the 1825 *East Florida Herald* stated that "The Dummetts lived in the McHardy house" (Halifax Historical Society 1957), it is more likely that they lived in Bunch's house. Recent archaeological research by Ted Payne has located the coquina foundation of the house and fireplace—as well as the slave settlement depicted on the 1819 map of Bunch's property—to the west of the sugar works and house site (Payne and Griffin 2001:58–60).

Reportedly Dummett brought a steam boiler with him from Barbados (Stanton 1949; Bishop 1975:9). In 1825, Dummett commissioned Reuben Loring to construct a sugar works and rum distillery for him. One source suggests that Loring may have been modifying an existing sugar works dating from Bunch's ownership of the property (Bishop 1975:9), but both Dummett and Loring referred to the works as the "first" one being built (Patricia C. Griffin, anthropologist, personal communication 2001). Construction extended at least a year, apparently due to a series of changes instituted by Dummett, as well as a lack of experienced craftsmen and good materials. Ultimately a lawsuit resulted over Loring's complaints of nonpayment and the inferiority of the materials and workmanship he was required to use (Loring 1828).

Anna Dummett reported that her father produced "about fifty hogsheads of sugar a year, with a very small force" (qtd. in Bishop 1975:10). But in December 1835, the Dummett property, like most of the other plantations, was destroyed by Indians at the onset of the Second Seminole War. Although the Dummett family retained ownership of the property until an 1839 mortgage foreclosure, the complex was never reused, and it became the ruin it is today (Payne 1999:106).

Dummett Records. We are fortunate to have a few written records pertaining to the construction of Dummett's sugar works. As previously noted, Thomas Dummett apparently brought his steam engine from Barbados (Stanton 1949). Based on the relatively small size of the engine firebox on the south wall, this may have been a smaller vertical engine (Figure 31) rather than the larger engines used at later sugar works. During this time period, a Boulton and Watt 10-horsepower engine cost approximately £1,090; this was the most popular size prior to the introduction of the American-made high-pressure engine after 1820 (Satchell 1997:3, 6). Since Dummett reportedly brought his engine with him in 1824, it seems likely that his would have been the smaller Boulton and Watt–type engine. Presumably the grinding apparatus would have been scaled to match the engine.

In addition to the indication that Dummett was knowledgeable about sugar and rum making from his residence in Barbados, there are records associated with his contract with the builder, Reuben Loring, and Loring's subsequent suit against Dummett over lack of payment. Based on these records, Dummett also brought in a French sugar maker from Barbados, Monsieur Pursier (Humphries 1831).

One undated invoice from Loring, which anthropologist Patricia Griffin believes is from early in the project (Patricia C. Griffin, personal communication 2001), describes the construction as follows:

> A wall 50 feet long—22½ inches thick, perhaps 27 inches up to 7 feet
>   15 feet high independent of the foundation
> A ditto—50 feet long—18 inches thick—7 feet high independent of foundation.
> Wall & brick work with arches sufficient for hanging 7 kettles—& 2 large
>   & long chimnies [*sic*].
>
> For three hundred dollars including my services in going to Tomoka 2 or 3 times, for the instruction of the people in the making & firing bricks. (Loring ca. 1825)

The brick firing Loring refers to is presumably for bricks to line the kettle supports; "Berry's Premium Firebricks," identical to those found at McHardy, were purchased for the furnaces and flues. Archaeologist Ted Payne (1999:111) identified a possible brick kiln adjacent to the Tomoka River; this site may be the one Loring mentions in his bill.

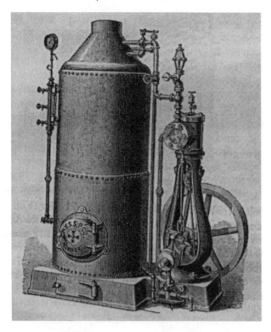

31. Illustration of a semi-portable steam engine, by Robert H. Thurston, 1878.

A tabulation from Loring in April 1826, mentions building a brick foundation underground (perhaps the fireboxes or flues), adding 35 inches of extra height to the sugar house, adding 37 inches to a chimney, building "2 abutments 2 perch [per chimney] in each 4 perches at $1.25 a perch—$5.00," and building three arches (for the kettles?) (Loring 1826). This invoice suggests that one chimney was a later addition, and that there was a total of two chimneys, based on the totals for the abutments and the earlier invoice. A deposition in the subsequent lawsuit mentions that Loring modified "the bell of the kettles to keep the liquor from boiling out" at the request of the sugar striker, Monsieur Pursier (Humphries 1831).

Describing the situation in which he was involved, Loring stated in his deposition, "the said Reuben [Loring] was generally delayed and hindered with his workmen and from want of the said materials properly hindered & exposed to great expense and lots of time to the great damage" (Loring 1826). One of Loring's masons confirmed that "the plan of the sugar mill was changed" (Barlow 1826), while another stated that "the changes of plan made the work greater, quantity of time greater" and that Dummett "was sometimes deficient in materials" (Humphries 1831).

One other description of the sugar works comes from the reminiscences of Anna Dummett, daughter of the property owner. Anna stated that "In connection with the sugar house there was a large distillery. . . . On the way to the distillery there were three large cisterns into which the molasses from the sugar house ran.

These cisterns held between two and three hundred gallons each. They were sunk in the ground, the covers made of boards supported by beams, being level with the path" (Dummett 1849:9–10). She seems to be describing the purgery. On one occasion young Anna fell into a vat after the head slave had rigged the boards to deter Indians working on the plantation from stealing rum (Dummett 1949:9–10). It is not presently clear where these cisterns were located at the sugar works, since the distillery is immediately adjacent to the boiling train rather than in a separate building. Anna Dummett may have been referring to a separate purgery and/or a storehouse for filled barrels.

Thomas Dummett apparently got along reasonably well with the local Seminole, as he employed some of them on his plantation. Anna Dummett reported that approximately 40 Indians worked on the property during the harvest and grinding season (Dummett 1949:9–10). As she said: "The Indians [Seminole], were constantly on and around the plantation. They supplied us with game and were always glad to take sugar or clothing of some kind in exchange; they were glad to get silver but would never receive paper money. They would always help themselves to molasses or cane, but this was done openly, and we never knew them to steal anything but a small piece of lead pipe which projected from the distillery" (Dummett 1949:9–10). This did not deter the Seminole from destroying Dummett's plantation at the outbreak of the Second Seminole War, after the Dummett family had retreated to St. Augustine for safety (Strickland 1957:5–13).

Post-Dummett Ownership. The destruction of Dummett's plantation plus the loss of some of his slaves to the Indians forced him to sell his remaining slaves, and in 1837, he lost his plantation through a mortgage foreclosure (Strickland 1957:9; Payne and Griffin 2001:67). By the 1940s, Dummett was part of E. B. Smoaks's property (Daniel et al. 1980:113).

During the early twentieth century, Dummett, like Cruger-DePeyster in New Smyrna Beach, was erroneously identified as a Spanish mission site, San Antonio de Anacape. Research determined, however, that the actual location of the Anacape mission was on the St. Johns River (Milanich 1995:176), and that there were no missions south of St. Augustine (Gannon 1965:64). In addition, none of the Spanish missions outside of St. Augustine were masonry. Combined with the extensive written records describing the construction of the sugar works and the subsequent lawsuit between Loring and Dummett, it is somewhat amazing that this myth was ever accepted.

The Dummett Sugar Works

The primary feature of the Dummett site is the sugar works itself (Figures 32 and 33). There are bricks and coquina block located approximately 45 feet northeast of the sugar house, suggesting the possible presence of a second structure.

32. Looking northeast at Dummett sugar works.

Interpreting the Site. The Dummett site is somewhat difficult to interpret due to its condition. There has been extensive collapse and/or removal of the masonry, and the site has been partially covered by both earth and vegetation. Examination of the ruins, however, supports the indication from the historic record that there were a number of changes in the sugar works during or after its initial construction. The following descriptions are based on the 2001 study (Wayne et al. 2001) and drawings by archaeologist John Griffin (1952a).

The extant sugar works remains consist of portions of the north wall, the sugar train and distillery, two chimneys, the balance of the foundation walls, and two wells (Figure 34). Substantial deterioration has occurred since the early twentieth century (Figures 35 and 36) and since it was documented in 1952 by John Griffin (Figure 37). It is not clear if the entire main building was masonry construction, since Loring's records reference building only three masonry walls and two chimneys (Loring ca. 1825). Two walls are visible in the older photographs, but given the lack of visible masonry remains around the site, it may be that part of the structure was wood on a substantial masonry foundation. Dummett seems to have been one of the first sugar works in East Florida to use extensive masonry, with the massive Bulow sugar works in southeastern Flagler County being built during the same time period.

There is some uncertainty as to whether there was a third chimney at Dummett. Griffin's (1952a) drawing (Figure 37) indicates that he located the base for a third

33. Looking southwest at Dummett sugar works.

chimney, and there are markings on the remaining north wall indicating possible spacing for a chimney. However, Payne (Ted M. Payne, archaeologist, personal communication 2001) did not find a chimney base during his archaeological testing at this site (Payne 1999), and only two chimneys are present in the older photographs (Figures 35 and 36). It is not clear what function or purpose a third chimney would serve. The 2001 study speculated that the building could have been erected originally as a four-kettle train with a chimney, and then later expanded to add another kettle and the distillery (Wayne et al. 2001:72). In addition to a chimney for the distillery, such an expansion might have required a new chimney at the end of an expanded kettle row. It should be noted, however, that Griffin (1952a) showed only four kettles and a clarifier. Recent examination of the remains suggest there were actually five kettles in the final configuration (Figure 34), and a worker's deposition during the lawsuit said that the plans called for five kettles (Van Horn 1826). Loring (ca. 1825) refers to "arches sufficient for hanging 7 kettles," but this probably included the two distillery vessels.

Alternatively, a three-chimney setup could have consisted of a chimney for the distillery and a chimney for the sugar train (the existing two chimneys), plus a third chimney for the steam engine, with under-the-floor flues extending from the engine on the south wall to the chimney on the north wall. This would be a very sophisticated construction system, which would also probably be unnecessary with the relatively small engine expected at a site of this period. Ultimately, however,

DUMMETT SUGAR MILL AND DISTILLERY, 8Vo241
TOMOKA BASIN GEOPARK

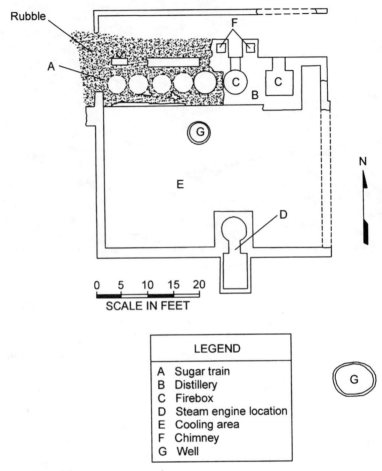

Rubble

A

F

C
C

B

G

N

E

D

0 5 10 15 20
SCALE IN FEET

LEGEND

A   Sugar train
B   Distillery
C   Firebox
D   Steam engine location
E   Cooling area
F   Chimney
G   Well

G

34. Plan of Dummett sugar works.

there is no apparent reason to have a third chimney on the north wall at this operation, and the only clear statements in Loring's (ca. 1825, 1826) records refer to two
chimneys.

The Existing Sugar Works Remains. The existing coquina ruins delimit an almost
square two-room structure. The construction is random ashlar coquina in which
the stones are sawn, tooled, and laid either in regular courses or randomly. There is
no direct access between the two rooms, and it has not been determined whether
the smaller room had masonry walls above the footings. As a result, it is not clear
what function was served by the room on the north side of the sugar train, other

35. Interior of Dummett sugar works, ca. 1935. (Courtesy of the Florida Memory Project, Florida State Archives, Tallahassee)

than providing access to the fireboxes and perhaps functioning as a storage area. It seems small to have been the purgery, particularly considering the lack of direct access between the spaces. In addition, Anna Dummett's (1949) descriptions suggest the purgery may have been in a separate building with subsurface molasses tanks.

On the south exterior of the existing ruins, there is a coquina block–lined well with traces of stucco on its interior walls. Presumably this well served the nearby steam engine. The grinder was probably located in this area in proximity to the engine. It seems likely that there would have at least been a pole-supported roof over the grinder to protect the machinery and allow work to continue in inclement weather.

The small steam engine firing pit and support are a combination of coquina and brick (Figure 38). The north chamber on the interior of the building has a brick support and round interior, suggesting it held the boiler. The square exterior chamber wall may have been plastered. The firebox extends to the south of the foundation walls of the ruin with a thick firebrick arch aligned with the building foundation separating it from the north chamber.

The south side of the interior of the ruins would have functioned as the cooling area for the crystallizing sugar, while the train and distillery are located against the north wall. The building remains themselves rest on a random ashlar coquina

36. Exterior of Dummett sugar works, ca. 1935. (Courtesy of the Florida Memory Project, Florida State Archives, Tallahassee)

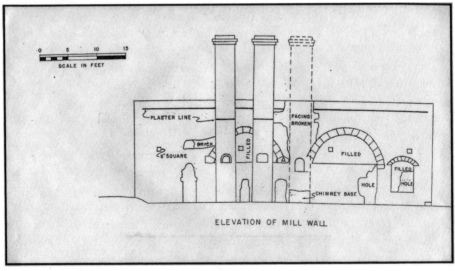

37. Elevation of Dummett sugar works, by John W. Griffin, 1952. (Courtesy of Patricia C. Griffin, St. Augustine, Florida)

38. Engine firebox at Dummett sugar works.

foundation on a 20-inch-thick footing that continues around all sides. The lower portion of the extant wall has smaller, loosely dressed blocks with wide mortar joints, while the upper portion has well-trimmed large blocks with smaller, tooled joints. Larger joints are often chinked with small fragments of coquina and brick. Striations in the coquina indicate both weathering and the use of an iron rod in quarrying, in which the rod is inserted in the soft stone to break off pieces. The wall was originally plastered on both interior and exterior with tabby plaster. Pockets on the interior of the north wall with traces of plaster indicate that rough-hewn wood beams were present to support the equipment (Figure 32). Based on shadow lines on the two chimneys, there was a gable roof on the one-story building; these marks are consistent with Loring's (ca. 1825) description of a 15-foot-high wall.

Two large coquina arches and one small arch were originally built into the north wall (Figures 37 and 39). When looking north, the eastern arch began at the side of the wall separating the distillery fireboxes and extended to the east end of the sugar train. The second arch began at the west end of the eastern arch and continued across the north wall behind the sugar train where it met a small arch at the west end of the train. The arches rested on piers that go directly to the footing; they appear to have been filled in immediately upon construction. Based on this construction, they were probably intended to be weight-relieving arches for the masonry wall. These may be the arches Loring (1826) referred to in his final bill.

39. Wall arch at Dummett sugar works.

The interior of the south room contains a second coquina-lined well to serve the sugar train and distillery (Figure 34). As with the exterior well, this well was stuccoed on the interior, corbeling slightly toward the top. This well is only four feet from the sugar train; as at McHardy, the close proximity suggests a narrow workers' platform for the train.

The distillery remains consist of two fireboxes that are adjacent, but not attached, to the interior of the north wall (Figure 34). Flues for the boxes were cut through the upper wall after it was built, suggesting one of the plan changes noted in the construction records. The eastern firebox has coquina outer walls with a brick interior forming a curved support for the distillery pot. A lip on the interior probably supported a grating for the fire. A 20-inch-thick coquina wall separates the two fireboxes. The western box has a round interior formed from both red brick and firebrick in a rowlock pattern on edge, sometimes with just the narrow (header) end of the brick exposed.

The sugar train is located immediately west of the distillery fireboxes with a flue entering the wall adjacent to the west chimney. Both flue and chimney are brick lined, apparently to the top of the chimney. Presumably there was a narrow platform on the south side of the train. There are also bricked-in flues on the south side of the sugar train. The presence of these flues at what would have been the workers' platform suggests a change in the layout of the train during the construction process. Perhaps the train was initially constructed as a Spanish train and then changed to a more sophisticated Jamaica train.

Based on brick-lined circular areas in the top of the train, there were five kettles. The train tapers slightly to the west where the final kettle, the *teche,* would have been located. The south wall of the train is very thick, and there is a battered (sloping) wall functioning as a buttress at the west end of the train. This is also the location of the firebox for the train. The tabby mortar in the train tends to have large oyster-shell inclusions, as well as chinking with brick and coquina fragments. The joints are wide buttered joints, or joints with thick mortar that has not been pointed or trimmed. This is particularly true in the lower area, which corresponds to the footing of the eastern part of the building.

The narrow north room provides access to the fireboxes of the chimneys and distillery. Vertical scribing on the north side of the standing wall marks the chimney limits; a set of similar marks are present west of the existing chimneys. These marks may have suggested the presence of a third chimney to Griffin (1952a). The western chimney has a brick lining, which begins at the cleanout level of the chimney, with coquina below the lining. At the junction of the coquina and brick, the mortar contains small fragments of broken glass—perhaps with some thought of strengthening the mortar.

Both chimneys are double corbeled at the top (Figures 32 and 33). The western chimney ties into the north wall only at the top of the existing wall. The wall side of the chimney is brick to above the top of the wall, where it switches to coquina. The eastern chimney cleanout contains marked Berry firebricks identical to those found at McHardy. This chimney is tied into the north building wall from the footing to the top of the wall, indicating that both were built at the same time. The difference in construction of the two chimneys in relation to the wall indicates that the western chimney was added after most of the wall and the eastern chimney had been built. This means it is the chimney Loring was asked to add during construction. It also supports the theory that the sugar train may have been begun as a Spanish train, which was then modified to a Jamaica train with a continuous flue and chimney.

An opening on the north side of the wall behind the sugar train provides access to the flue between the *grande* and *flambeau* kettles, perhaps for a supplemental fire. Fireboxes for the distillery are located between the chimneys and east of the eastern chimney. The western firebox has a large block of coquina as a lintel, while the eastern box has a smaller arched opening with a metal lintel between the arch and lower chamber. The flue for the eastern distillery firebox, which was cut through the wall after construction, has a cast-iron bar at its base and a cast-iron plate embedded in the eastern chimney where the flue enters. These were presumably inserted for reinforcement when the flue was cut through the wall. Firebrick from the chimney extends into the flue.

Overall, the masonry on the north side of the north wall is better quality than that on the interior. Perhaps less care was taken on the interior because it would be behind the processing equipment. In addition, both interior and exterior were plastered or stuccoed, hiding any defects.

Dummett Summary. While not large, the complex masonry construction reflects the value that Dummett invested in his sugar works, as does the presence of a steam engine to power the crushing operation. Obviously Dummett felt that sugar was going to be a lucrative product on his plantation, along with rum; thus he used the latest technology and erected a building that was meant to endure. The structure also clearly reflects the numerous changes recorded by its builder, Reuben Loring, and perhaps the process of adapting to a new technology—steam.

Rees Spring Garden

The Rees Spring Garden plantation is located at DeLeon Springs State Park on the west side of Volusia County (Figure 1). The remains of the sugar works have been incorporated into the existing pancake restaurant at the springs (Figure 40). The park is open daily from 8 a.m. to sunset, and the pancake restaurant is open until 5 p.m. every day. Park information is available at www.floridastateparks.org/deleonsprings.

The chimney for the sugar train is now the chimney for the restaurant, and the remains of the train extend out the back of the building. The waterwheel and gears have been incorporated into the springs side of the building. The existing waterwheel is a recent replacement for the original. Kettles and pieces of sugar works machinery are sitting within a small roofed pavilion adjacent to the sugar train, and the axle with portions of the spokes of the original wheel have been mounted adjacent to an explanatory sign.

Until 1995, previous research at DeLeon Springs focused on the prehistoric Native American occupation of the area. At that time Ellis Archaeology/Gulf Archaeology Research Institute completed an archaeological survey of the park. This study included documentation of the sugar works remains, but focused primarily on the prehistoric resources within the park (Denson et al. 1995). The 2001 stabilization study by SouthArc, Inc., updated the drawings completed in 1995 (Wayne et al. 2001). The most extensive work at the site was completed in 2002 by Patricia Griffin and by Ted Payne of American Preservation Consultants, Inc. Griffin completed an in-depth historic study of the property, and Payne conducted archaeological testing around the sugar works with partial excavation of the sugar train ruins (Griffin 2002; Payne 2002).

History of Spring Garden

Spring Garden at DeLeon Springs was developed by William Williams and Maj. Joseph Woodruff. Under the ownership of Col. Orlando Rees, it was known as Garden Spring (later called Spring Gardens) (Payne and Griffin 2001:115, 117).

40. Looking northeast at Rees Spring Garden sugar works.

Legends. A number of legends have been reported concerning the early settlement of DeLeon Springs, although recent research by Patricia Griffin has demonstrated that these stories lack veracity. One tale, common to many Florida springs, attributes the European discovery of DeLeon Springs to Ponce de Leon in the early sixteenth century (Burt 1929:10). Another source suggests that the first settlement was made by the Spaniards in 1570 when they cleared 100 acres for sugar cane and built a mill (Francke et al. 1986:201). But recent research by Griffin (2002:7) determined that during the First Spanish Period, the area of the springs was unoccupied and was identified as land not granted by the Crown.

A final source claims that the first documented settlement was made by Greeks and Minorcans under the direction of Gen. James Oglethorpe of Georgia at the beginning of the British Period to produce indigo (Denson et al. 1995:37). The settlers were reported to have been massacred by Indians by the end of the British Period in 1783 (Denson et al. 1995:37). This story seems to blend the British Turnbull Minorcan settlers in New Smyrna Beach with various Indian raids at DeLeon Springs. There is no evidence that either Oglethorpe or the Minorcans were at DeLeon Springs (Patricia C. Griffin, anthropologist, personal communication 2001). In fact, in 1779, during the time of the supposed Oglethorpe settlement, two 500-acre tracts that included the springs were granted to William Panton and James Forbes, Indian traders (Griffin 2002:9). There may have been a trading post there, as a band of Creek Indians was reported to have been living at Spring Garden in 1789 (Dunbar 1980). However, Griffin's recent research was unable to confirm that Panton or Forbes conducted any substantial activity at the springs (Griffin 2002:11).

Williams Ownership. At the beginning of the Second Spanish Period, the Crown offered grants to those who would profess loyalty to the king and convert to Catholicism. After seven years of little success in this endeavor, the Spanish Crown changed to a grant system that required grantees to bring or purchase slaves and cattle for their plantations (Griffin 2002:11). Many of the people who took advantage of this offer were Loyalists who had fled to Florida and the Bahamas as a result of the Revolutionary War. William Williams and his brother Samuel immigrated from the Bahamas to Florida in 1803, with Samuel initially settling near Daytona Beach, and William in part of the former Turnbull Grant in New Smyrna Beach. When William Williams's Turnbull tract proved unproductive, he asked to exchange this grant for better land. He was then granted 2,020 acres near the St. Johns River, which he named Spring Garden. This acreage encompassed the previous Panton and Forbes grants. William Williams produced cotton, corn, and other provision crops on his new lands, while still farming 80 acres of his original grant near New Smyrna. He died in 1808, leaving his property to his three nephews (Griffin 2002:13).

The Williams family continued to work the Spring Garden plantation until the Patriot War of 1812, in which William Williams II was fervently on the side of the Patriots. It appears that Spring Garden was managed by an overseer, Mr. Burgess, during the war. The plantation was apparently unharmed due to the Williams connection to the Patriots (Griffin 2002:16).

Woodruff Ownership. After the United States acquired Florida in 1821, Joseph and Jane Woodruff acquired what was described as the "undivided third of the original Spring Garden Plantation" (Griffin 2002:18). At that point Spring Garden was listed as approximately 6,173 acres. Jane Woodruff described their new plantation as 2,020 acres, the size of the original Williams grant. James M. Fitch bought another part of the original Spring Garden the same year, although his deed was not filed until 1887 (Griffin 2002:18–19).

Maj. Joseph Woodruff was from McIntosh County, Georgia (Griffin 2002:18), and his wife was from Charleston, South Carolina. Woodruff may have been familiar with sugar cultivation in both coastal Georgia and South Carolina. However, initially the Woodruffs planted cotton and raised livestock. They also traded with a band of Euchee Indians who had occupied the property prior to the Woodruffs' arrival (Griffin 2002:21).

The Woodruffs lived very simply on their new plantation in what is known as a dogtrot house—a log house consisting of two rooms connected by an open central passageway. In an 1838 narrative, Jane Woodruff described her "wig-wam" as having two rooms, one used by the family and the other for eating. The overseer and the Woodruffs' three nephews slept in the dining room (Griffin 2002:19). When guests came to the plantation, Jane Woodruff had beds made up in the cotton warehouse (Griffin 2002:19).

During the first summer after their settlement, the plantation and its occupants, including the animals, were struck with disease. The combination of disease and a lack of supplies led to the deaths of many of the people and most of the livestock. When colder weather set in, the situation improved and Woodruff's crops thrived (Griffin 2002:22–23). By 1827, Woodruff was described as "one of the largest and most valuable planters on the east of the Suwannee" with immense crops (Carter 1962:23:899).

In 1828, Woodruff decided to produce sugar. He traveled to New York to acquire steam equipment but died in Charleston on his way back. His wife and family abandoned the Spring Garden plantation after his death (Griffin 2002:23).

Rees Ownership. By the 1830 census, the area encompassing the springs was owned by Colonel Orlando Rees. Rees was also from South Carolina, and probably acquired the property after Woodruff's death. Rees, owner of more than 90 slaves, was determined to produce sugar (Griffin 2002:24). Rees called his plantation Garden Spring, although it was also referred to as Spring Gardens (Payne and Griffin 2001:117). The artist John James Audubon, who visited in 1832, said the cane was grown "on the borders of a lake . . . having been reclaimed from swampy land of a black colour, rich and very productive" (qtd. in Proby 2002:311).

When Rees heard of an engineer who was helping planters along the Tomoka with their sugar works, he invited him to Spring Garden. It is possible that this engineer was Duncan Macrae who, with his brother, built a sugar works at the former Addison plantation. The artist John James Audubon was touring Florida in 1831 to collect water birds for his *Birds of America* series (Porter 2009). While visiting Bulow Plantation during this period, he wrote of going to the "McCreigh" plantation (Griffin 2002:24).

Audubon and the unnamed engineer arrived at the springs in 1832. Observing the flow of the springs, the engineer decided to use waterpower to run the mill. He built an undershot wheel, the only one known in Florida (Griffin 2002:24). The pool was dammed and a spillway was constructed to divert water to the wheel (Dunbar 1980). According to Audubon, the Spring Garden plantation produced cotton, corn, and sugar, with the mill at the springs (Audubon 1879:228). Presumably the mill was effective in grinding cane, since Rees had "cane sufficient to manufacture ninety hogshead of sugar" from his property, according to war participant Woodburne Potter (qtd. in Griffin 2002:32).

Rees apparently lived in the old Woodruff house, as no other residence is shown on an 1834 map of the plantation. Tradition and Audubon's account of his visit suggest that the slave quarters were located at the eastern edge of the plantation. Audubon described them as "huts" (qtd. in Griffin 2002:27).

In 1835, at the outbreak of the Second Seminole War, Rees's plantation was among those destroyed. An 1836 account in the *East Florida Herald* says, "The plantation laid waste, and the buildings and thirty-five hogsheads of sugar, and the cane sufficient to manufacture seventy hogsheads more destroyed; and the Negroes, amounting to one hundred and sixty and horse, and mules taken off. Loss about $130,000" (qtd. in Griffin 2002:32). U.S. troops moved to Spring Garden in mid-March 1836, finding a hastily abandoned Seminole village (Dunbar 1980). The Indians returned after the soldiers departed, retaining control of the springs until 1838, when Gen. Zachary Taylor set up an encampment northeast of the springs (Denson et al. 1995:41).

Post–Seminole War. Spring Garden was abandoned for several years until it was purchased from Rees's heir by Thomas Starke. Starke rebuilt the old mill and enlarged it, adding cotton gins (Griffin 2002:34). Apparently Starke continued to produce sugar, planting 12 acres of cane on newly cleared land with only 12 slaves. In 1850 he claimed he was averaging 2,500 pounds of high-quality sugar per acre—500 pounds more than the Florida average—and that he was getting 6½ gallons of juice from 12 stalks of cane (Smith 1973:68). Starke operated a thriving plantation for several years. He died in the early 1850s, but his son John continued to operate the plantation, again refurbishing the mill and adding corn grinders (Griffin 2002:35).

John Starke provided provisions to Confederate forces during the Civil War. In 1864, Union soldiers under Col. William Birney came to Spring Garden in an effort to capture Starke. They noted that the spring was "running out with such force that it carries a grist-mill and extensive cotton gins, and yet appears capable of doing more" (Dickison 1962:171). Local lore says that the Union troops dismantled the gristmill, throwing it into the springs (Griffin 2002:37). Another account says that Colonel Nobel's Union troops "demolished everything except the frame of the old mill, the water wheel, chimney and arches [sugar train]. All the houses, stores and fences were once again burned" (Francke et al. 1986:204).

The mill was again rebuilt in 1878 by Maj. George Norris of New York, who bought the property in 1872. Norris planted extensive citrus groves in the area and established a settlement for northerners at the springs. He built a hotel, the Spring Garden House, adjacent to the springs itself (Griffin 2002:39).

By the 1880s, the springs had become a small tourist resort operated first by De Leon Springs Company and later by the Volusia County Bank (Warren 1989:6). Extensive development of the springs facilities occurred after 1886 when the railroad connected DeLeon Springs to Jacksonville, Tampa, and Key West. This development continued into the early years of the twentieth century, when a casino and hotel were built. Later, the Clyde Beatty circus wintered at DeLeon Springs. In 1920 the spring was dammed as a power source for the local area, causing it to back up and flood the area beyond the spillway. After local residents blocked the spring run, the water flow returned to the spillway (Denson et al. 1995:42).

The park was again revamped in 1953 as a tourist attraction under the ownership of George Thoferhn. In 1982, the property was sold to the State of Florida and became a state park, its present function (Denson et al. 1995:42). The following description of the sugar works is based on the 2001 study (Wayne et al. 2001) and the recent research by Payne (2002).

Spring Garden Sugar Works

Today the Spring Garden sugar works have been partly incorporated into the modern restaurant (Figure 40). The old sugar works extends out of the rear of the restaurant, while the chimney end is inside the building. The existing waterwheel is a modern nonfunctioning replica of the original. A second chimney added to the restaurant duplicates the shape and appearance of the original chimney, although it is smaller in scale.

The Mill. Photographs taken in the late nineteenth century show the mill wheel first leaning, and eventually lying almost on the ground (Figure 41). Sometime after 1913, the wheel was realigned and its wooden supports were replaced with concrete (Denson et al. 1995:61). The deteriorated concrete supports and wheel were replaced in 1999 with the present reproduction (Figure 42). Gears and wheels associated with the transfer of power from the mill wheel to the corn grinder remain on the interior of the restaurant.

Prior to its reconstruction, the mill wheel was recorded as being approximately 26 feet in diameter (Denson et al. 1995:62), with 28 spokes. Since Thomas Spalding's Georgia water mill had a 24-foot wheel (Eubanks 2004), it seems reasonable to assume that Rees's mill would produce comparable power—approximately equivalent to a 10-horsepower engine, the typical size used at steam-powered mills. This, as well as the late-1820s to 1830s date of the Rees sugar works, would suggest that a horizontal mill was used at Spring Garden. The Rees mill wheel is an undershot wheel in which the water passes beneath the wheel, pushing the lower paddles to create the motion. Since the spring is not tidal, but flows constantly, presumably the mill would have been functional 24 hours a day if necessary. Based on the location of the waterwheel and its extant gears (Figure 43), the mill itself would have been where the present restaurant is located, between the wheel and the sugar train.

The Sugar Train. In its last incarnation, the sugar train was a Jamaica train built of brick. The portion exposed at the rear of the restaurant would have held four kettles, one of which is still in place (Figures 43 and 44). Part of the fifth kettle and the connection to the chimney lie under the porch of the restaurant. According to park staff, the section connecting to the chimney has largely been removed. The brickwork is badly deteriorated, primarily as a result of a large oak tree which grew out of the junction between the *grande* and *flambeau* kettles. Much of the south side of the train has been destroyed.

41. Spring Garden waterwheel in late nineteenth century. (Courtesy of the Florida Memory Project, Florida State Archives, Tallahassee)

42. Spring Garden modern waterwheel.

REES SPRING GARDEN, 8Vo30
DELEON SPRINGS STATE PARK, FLORIDA

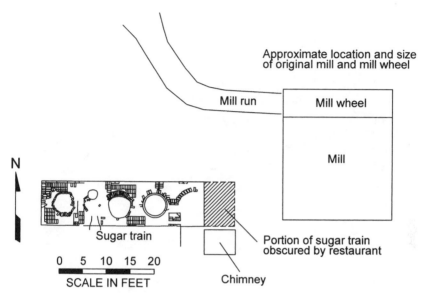

43. Plan of Spring Garden sugar works.

44. South side of Spring Garden sugar train.

45. Spring Garden, ca. 1912. (Courtesy of the Florida Memory Project, Florida State Archives, Tallahassee)

Variations in the brick and mortar attest to the sequence of rebuilding that this facility has undergone. Recent archaeological testing revealed that the brick was initially English common bond, but when the west side was rebuilt, Liverpool bonding was used (Payne 2002:19–20). The latter has three rows of stretchers separated by a row of headers (McKee 1973:79). Payne speculates that the workers would have stood on the ground on the north side of the train and that the purgery would have been to the west (Payne 2002:19). The poor condition of the train makes it almost impossible to determine the locations of the fireboxes or any flues. Presumably the firebox was located at the west end of the train opposite the chimney.

As previously noted, the train's chimney still stands and has been incorporated into the kitchen of the restaurant. Park staff reported that the chimney was repointed and an iron exterior frame added between 1982 and 1988. As it presently stands, the chimney is square, tapering up to the height of the present restaurant gable, where it steps in and continues up as a square chimney for about one-third the height of the lower portion (Figure 40). The smaller, modern chimney is located to the north.

Spring Garden Summary. Although the present form of the Rees sugar works is deceptive, the original complex was a frame building with the waterwheel driving the crusher on the north end, and the Jamaica train on the southwest side. It is not clear whether this would have been one large rectangular building or an L-shaped structure, although late-nineteenth-century photographs show a building that excludes the sugar train, putting it outside (Figure 45). The most important aspect of the Rees complex is the use of waterpower to drive the crusher—the only example of this system known in East Florida.

Summary of Adaptive Sugar Works

In McHardy's final form and in Dummett, we see the evolution from the Spanish train with its individual fireboxes to the Jamaica train with a single continuous flue. At Dummett, we see the introduction of the steam engine, which revolutionized the crushing of the cane. But Dummett, with its many construction alterations, also reflects the trials and errors involved in adopting new technologies.

At Rees Spring Garden, we have the sole example in the East Florida sugar works of an alternative to steam- or animal-powered crushing: the waterwheel. This has to be considered a somewhat experimental operation in this region, particularly given that it used a spring for the water source rather than a river or stream.

8
The Fully Evolved Sugar Works
Bulow, Macrae, Cruger-DePeyster, and Dunlawton

A first view of the [Cruger-DePeyster] ruins rarely fails to impress the thoughtful beholder with its great size and the large sum of money and months' [*sic*] of labor that evidently were expended in its construction and equipment.

—Capt. Charles H. Coe, *Debunking the So-Called Spanish Mission near New Smyrna Beach, Volusia County, Florida* (1941)

By the late 1820s to early 1830s, sugar production had reached its ultimate antebellum form on Florida plantations. The Jamaica train, steam engine, and horizontal mill were all in widespread use in the Caribbean sugar countries, which heavily influenced Florida. Under the leadership of men like Moses Levy, Thomas Dummett, and the Bulows in the mid- to late 1820s, sugar was identified as the ideal plantation product for East Florida. Records from the Territorial Period indicate that sugar was the primary crop on eight of the major plantations in the region: Bulow, Woodruff, Rees, Thomas Dummett, Macrae, Cruger and DePeyster, Anderson, and Douglas Dummett (Thomas's son who lived on Merritt Island) (Griffin 1999:7). This was a switch from the dominance of cotton during the Second Spanish Period (Griffin 1999:7).

The sugar works of East Florida reached their final stage during this period, that of fully evolved, steam-powered masonry structures. It should be noted that, in the Caribbean, "Enclosure of operations within masonry structures makes it first appearance in the late-17th century, as sugar manufacturing transitions to production at factory scale" (Meniketti 2006:63). This is the same transition that was made in Florida in the early nineteenth century.

Not only the sugar process but the structures themselves owed much to their Caribbean and Georgia predecessors in terms of architecture. These were large, substantial masonry buildings, often with fine architectural details indicating the hand of expert masons. The layouts were designed for maximum efficiency of production, as well as to provide security for both the expensive equipment and the valuable end products. The four sugar works addressed in this chapter vary in plan, but all encompassed a steam-powered horizontal mill, a Jamaica train, and a relatively large purgery. In one case (Dunlawton), there are two trains with a complex underground flue system, and in another case (Bulow), there are two purgeries to serve the sugar works.

A recent study of Caribbean sites showed that, as in Florida, the sugar works varied not only from island to island, but from plantation to plantation (Meide 2003). They could consist of a complex of separate buildings for each stage of the process, or be a single large structure with different rooms for the process. Archaeologist Chuck Meide's survey indicates that "The most common setup encountered was a main complex of two to three rooms, with an adjacent animal or wind mill. Mills seem to have usually been housed in a separate structure, if they were in an actual structure at all" (Meide 2003:24, 26). It should be noted that steam-powered mills were almost always enclosed by a building, probably due to the more complex and expensive equipment. Most Caribbean complexes had wells (Meide 2003:58), as do the East Florida examples, since water was vital to the process.

In terms of location within the property, proximity to the shipping point and to the cane fields seemed to be the dominant considerations. The planters' houses in the Caribbean were either near the sugar complex or "on a prominent upland position where it looked down upon the various aspects of the sugar-making endeavor" (Meide 2003:58). In East Florida, the sugar works are near either the King's Road or the rivers. Interestingly, the planters' houses do not seem to be near the sugar works in East Florida, and, of course, there is no upland position that would allow one to observe the entire property. There does seem to be a tendency to put the sugar works at a distance from the slave cabins on the plantations where both areas have been identified (Dummett, Bulow, Spring Garden, and possibly Dunlawton). This decision may have been made in an effort to limit the slaves' access to the products.

These buildings represented substantial investments to the planters. In 1822, a steam-powered sugar mill could cost as much as $12,000. By 1831, the price had dropped to $4,500 (Sitterson 1953:138), but even that was a costly enterprise at that period. The Bulow family valued their sugar works at $40,000 in their claims after its destruction in the Second Seminole War (Cresap 1982:157). As Meide (2003:7) points out, "planters accumulated substantial debts to commission agents and factors who marketed their produce and serviced their plantations and to slave traders who supplied their labor. . . . But profits could be immense, and many planters became extraordinarily wealthy." It is little wonder, then, that the planters invested the effort to make these buildings not only strong but reflective of their value to the plantation. It would have been immediately obvious to any visitor that these complexes were the centerpieces of the plantations—and equally obvious that the products were valuable commodities.

The four sugar complexes discussed in this chapter are fully evolved masonry sugar works. With the exception of Dunlawton, the last of the sugar works to operate in this area, there is little or no indication of experimentation or adaptation during the construction of these complexes. The builders clearly knew what they were doing and how to achieve their goals. In some cases, there is documentation that experienced engineers were involved in the construction and operation of these sugar works. It is probable that this was the case even in the sugar works that lack such documentation. Interestingly, these engineers seem to have been Scotsmen, but they clearly were familiar with Caribbean sugar works and probably gained their experience in the islands.

Bulow Plantation

Bulow Plantation is located at the southeastern tip of Flagler County in Bulow Plantation Ruins State Historic Park (Figure 1). The park is open Thursday through Monday from 9 a.m. to 5 p.m., and can be reached from Old Dixie Highway via Old King's Road (CR 2001). Park information can be found at www.floridastateparks.org/bulowcreek.

The site consists of the remains of the sugar works, a spring house foundation, the site of Bulow's plantation home, boat slips, and archaeological remains of slave cabins. Thanks to the excellent work of architect Herschel Shepard in 1967 (Daniel et al. 1980), the sugar works remains are well preserved and there is a small but excellent interpretative display, as well as demonstration plots of the primary plantation crops.

Preliminary archaeological studies were completed at Bulow Plantation by John W. Griffin (1952b). In 1967, extensive stabilization of the sugar works and implementation of interpretative exhibits were undertaken by Herschel Shepard. Limited archaeological testing was completed at this time to support the preservation efforts (Daniel et al. 1980; Gluckman and Baker 1967). Further archaeological studies were completed as part of the Halifax Plantation Development survey (Daniel et al. 1980). This study included drawings based largely on Griffin's earlier work and the 1967 restoration. The majority of the archaeology, however, has focused on the Bulow house site. The 2001 stabilization study by SouthArc, Inc., updated the 1967 drawings for the sugar works (Wayne et al. 2001).

This study will focus on the sugar works. This structure was built shortly after the Dummett sugar works discussed in the previous chapter, and at about the same time that Rees was constructing his water mill, since Bulow's engineer apparently designed Rees's water mill (Griffin 2002:24).

History of Bulow Plantation

"Bulowville" first appears as a 4,675-acre tract that was acquired in 1812 by James Russell, a shipwright of New Providence in the Bahamas. Reportedly Russell traded his 58-ton schooner, *Perseverance*, to the Spanish governor, Don Juan José de

Estrada, for the property. The schooner was valued at $2,300. He named his plantation "Good Retreat," but died within three years of its acquisition. His family did not occupy the property after his death, and apparently there were some issues over the title (Baker 1999:115; Wilson 1945:229).

Bulow Period. In 1820, Maj. Charles Wilhelm Bulow of Charleston acquired the property from Russell's son, James. Bulow was a wealthy South Carolina planter who had inherited an extensive fortune developed by his father and his grandfather, the Baron Joachim Von Bulow, in the early eighteenth century. Bulow continued to build on this fortune in Florida, acquiring a total of 6,000 acres on which he built Bulowville, described as "one of the finest plantations of his day, in this region" (Stanton 1949; Baker 1999:115). He cleared 1,500 acres for sugar cane, 1,000 for cotton, and smaller acreages for indigo and rice with the labor of 100 to 300 slaves (Stanton 1949; Bishop 1975:12).

Three years after acquiring Bulowville, Charles Bulow died, leaving the property to his son, John Joachim Bulow. John was still a minor, attending school in Paris, at the time of his father's death. He returned to Florida with his mother and adopted sister, managing the plantation under a trusteeship until he came of age (Stanton 1949).

Under the direction of the Bulows, a 2½-story main house was built on the creek. The house was 22 by 42 feet with 18-inch-thick masonry walls on the lower level on a coquina foundation; it probably had a frame upper story. It may have had an interior fireplace, as no evidence for an end fireplace was found. The structure allowed for two rooms on each floor, which were surrounded by a covered 10-foot-wide piazza on at least the lower level (Griffin 1952b).

In addition, the plantation included two kitchen buildings which were 20 by 20 feet in size (Gordon 2002:212), two cotton houses, the sugar works, 46 slave cabins in an arc near the main house, a sawmill, a corn house, stables, other outbuildings, and boat slips lined with discarded spirits bottles (Bishop 1975:12–13; Baker 1999:117). The arc of slave cabins, centered on the main house and about 150 yards from it, is an unusual configuration, known at only one other Florida plantation, Kingsley on Fort George Island in northeast Duval County. Limited archaeological investigation indicates that the cabins were small frame structures approximately 12 by 16 feet in size with wood floors, shingle roofs, and coquina-block foundations (Baker 1999:117–118; Daniel et al. 1980:71, 74–75).

John James Audubon was a guest of Bulow in 1831, leaving descriptions of Bulow's property and lifestyle, including the comment that an addition was being built at the sugar works (Stanton 1949). A plaque once located on the engine house read "Bulow Ville, Jan. 26th, 1831" (Wilson 1945:232); the plaque suggests the engine house was the addition Audubon mentioned. According to the 1830 census, Bulow operated his plantation during this period with 193 slaves (Florida Department of Environmental Protection 1998:29).

Like many of the planters in this region, John Bulow was on good terms with the Seminole Indians, who sometimes worked as laborers on the plantations, and regularly provided fresh meat to the planters (Dummett 1949:9–10; Bishop 1975:13; Wilson 1945:234–235). At the onset of the Second Seminole War in 1835, Bulow resisted when the Florida Militia's "Mosquito Roarers" under the command of Maj. Benjamin A. Putnam entered his property, even firing his four-pounder cannon (loaded with only powder and wadding) at the soldiers. In response, Putnam imprisoned Bulow and turned his house into a fortification. Failing in their efforts to subdue the Seminole and suffering from illness and injuries, Putnam, his soldiers, and the settlers retreated to St. Augustine in January 1836. On January 31, the Seminole destroyed Bulowville and the other plantations in the area; reportedly the fires from Bulowville could be seen 40 miles away in St. Augustine (Stanton 1949). On February 25, a military officer reported that "The noble mill and mansion are utterly destroyed" (Cohen 1964:143).

Too discouraged to rebuild his property, Bulow returned to Paris, where he died in 1836 at age 26 (Stanton 1949). When the executors for Bulow's estate filed a claim in 1839 for $40,000 in damages to the property, the claim was rejected by the Congressional Claims Committee because of Bulow's resistance to Major Putnam (Baker 1999:117).

Post–Seminole War. The estate passed to Bulow's mother and adopted sister and her family (Cardwell 1997:3). In 1869, the estate was partitioned among the eight Bulow heirs, although this decree was contested and not finalized until 1912. During this period, the property apparently remained undeveloped. In the following years, the parcels often changed hands, but little alteration was made. In 1945, the area containing the primary remains of Bulowville was acquired by the Volusia Hammock State Park Association and placed under the care of the Florida Board of Forestry and Parks, predecessor of the present Department of Environmental Protection. Bulow was placed on the National Register of Historic Places in 1970 (Daniel et al. 1980:170).

Bulow Sugar Works

The existing remains of the Bulowville sugar works consist of the large T-shaped boiling house–purgeries building, a separate engine house, two wells, and a spring house (Figure 46). The site originally included a frame sawmill operated by a steam engine; no visible evidence of this structure remains (Daniel et al. 1980:145). The following description is based on the 2001 stabilization study and the 1980 survey (Wayne et al. 2001; Daniel et al. 1980).

The T-shaped boiling house–purgeries may have been the largest of these facilities in East Florida, with an overall size of 93 by 119 feet (Daniel et al. 1980:145).

46. Looking west at Bulow sugar works.

Although the designer or engineer for the building is not known, it may have been the same Reuben Loring who built the Dummett sugar works (Daniel et al. 1980:146). Or it could have been Duncan Macrae, who later built the Macrae sugar works (Griffin 2002:24). In 1831, a Scottish engineer was an employee of John Bulow and escorted Bulow's guest, John Audubon, to the Rees Spring Garden plantation (Audubon 1879:228–231; Daniel et al. 1980:146). Although Audubon did not name the engineer, it could have been Macrae, since Audubon mentions visiting the "McCreigh" plantation (Griffin 2002:24). It seems unlikely that there would be many Scottish engineers familiar with sugar works operating at the same time in this small area. Audubon also noted that an addition was under construction at the Bulow mill during his visit in 1831. Presumably, the addition was built under the supervision of Bulow's engineer. In 1967, it was reported that John F. Stanton of Ormond Beach had a 1907 postcard that showed a metal plaque on the north exterior wall of the boiler room which stated "Bulow Ville January 26th, 1831" (Wilson 1945:232). (Note: A replacement plaque has recently been set into this wall.) A 1926 plan of the mill ruins showed another plaque above the middle arch of the second story which read "Bulowville _____ Nov. - 1838 - B.B.B." (Gluckman and Baker 1967:5). It is possible that the plaque dated 1831 refers to the addition under construction when Audubon visited. The date on the other plaque, however, falls after the mill was destroyed in the Second Seminole War. The investigation in 1967 did

BULOW, 8FL7
BULOW STATE PARK, FLORIDA

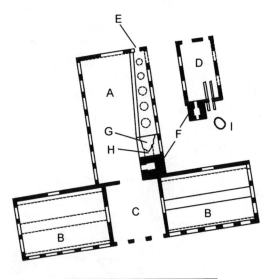

47. Plan of Bulow sugar works.

note that the west wall of the boiler room had a different construction than the rest of the mill, suggesting either a repair or construction in a piecemeal manner (Gluckman and Baker 1967:5).

This description of the extant remains begins with the engine house and continues through boiling house, work area, and purgeries, finishing with the second well and spring house (Figure 47). A concrete walkway with approximately knee-height chains leads visitors through the complex and deters access to the ruins (Figure 46). Signage identifies each part of the sugar works as well as the individual kettles within the boiling train. A dehumidified exhibit nearby has conceptual drawings of the sugar works as it may have looked prior to its destruction, artifacts from the Bulow site, and information on sugar production.

48. Looking north at Bulow engine house.

The Engine House. The engine house, like the main sugar works, is built of large random ashlar coquina block (Figures 48 and 49). The joints between the blocks are tight and well done; the buildings were probably plastered. The structure is 1½ stories tall with a 30-foot-high square tapering chimney at the southwest corner. An arched brick flue is located at the south base of the chimney (Figure 49). The chimney has exterior iron bands placed sometime before the 1967 stabilization. The building had a shingled gable roof with the ridge parallel to the long axis of the building, which paralleled the boiling house (Figure 47). The building's rectangular windows had wooden lintels and shutters. There is one window above the northwest entry and two on the west wall; most of the east wall of the engine house is missing, but it probably also had two windows. A brick and coquina framework on the east interior of the building extending out the south wall would have supported the engine/boiler equipment. A horizontal flue extends along the west wall with a furnace at the north end. It is possible that an exterior lean-to, possibly on the east wall, was present to protect the wood and bagasse used as fuel. A 14-foot-wide alley separates the engine house from the boiling house (Figure 47).

The boiler may have also powered the nearby sawmill to the east; there are no extant remains of this building. Architect Herschel Shepard says that the sawmill would probably have required a separate engine, partly because of the difficulty and complexity of remotely linking the sawmill to the engine for the crusher. A sawmill requires considerable space to feed the logs to the machinery. Sawmills from that

49. Northeast corner of Bulow engine house.

period operated up-and-down frame saws in which a walking beam transferred the motion of the steam piston to a flywheel, which in turn powered the saw. A walk-ing beam near the boiler house was partially exposed by visitors to Bulow during the 1967 stabilization; the beam was reburied and presumably remains in place to-day (Herschel Shepard, architect, personal communication 2008).

It is not clear where the cane mill was located. One description suggests that it was located upstairs in the engine house or on the upper floor of the boiling house (Daniel et al. 1980:131). Another more likely possibility is the space between the two structures (Gluckman and Baker 1967:11), as at Dunlawton. It should be noted that placement of the crusher upstairs in either structure raises questions as to the load-bearing capability of the upstairs floors as well as the practicality of not only transferring power to the crusher, but also raising the cane to the upper level, crushing it, and then removing the bagasse. An exterior location for this rather messy process makes more sense. Given that the mill would need to be near the machinery that drives it, but also close to the sugar train, a location between the two structures seems to be the most practical solution. As archaeologists Stephen Gluckman and Henry Baker (1967:11) have pointed out, this location would re-quire the use of a cane carrier (see Figure 9) due to the limited space between the structures.

A single well is located in the area south of the boiling house (Figure 47), al-though earlier plans show two wells in this location. The well has been filled, and

50. Looking southeast at Bulow boiling house.

only the coquina upper level is presently visible. Another large well is located north of the boiling house to serve the train and clarifier.

The Boiling House. The boiling house is located in the leg of the T-shaped sugar works (Figure 47), oriented north-south. Sugar planter John Cleland (1836:22) indicated that this orientation maximized protection of the train from northerly winds and winter storms. Little remains of the walls of this structure (Figure 50). The badly degraded five-kettle sugar train is located on the east wall. Based on the remaining wall portions, seven regularly spaced windows were located on the east and six on the west walls of this room to provide ventilation. Presumably these windows were fitted with wooden shutters. The floor of the boiling house was probably coquina, but this has not been determined (Daniel et al. 1980:150). A large rectangular window or door is located over the arched doorway to the adjacent storage and loading room. The presence of this door indicates that the attic level of the boiling house was accessible and may have been used for storage.

Like the engine house, the sugar works is built of coquina blocks. A larger tapering square chimney is located at the south end of the sugar train at the junction of the T-shaped structure (Figures 47 and 50). The firebox for the train is at the north end, and a platform for the clarifier sits above the flue to the chimney on the south end of the train. Presumably the coolers were located on the west side of the boiling room (Gluckman and Baker 1967:11).

Storage/Loading Room and Purgeries. A 30-foot square storage and loading room

51. South facade, Bulow storage/loading room.

is located on the south side of the boiling room connected by large brick segmentally arched openings to the boiling room and the two purgeries (Figure 47). A cold
joint between the storage room and the boiling house suggests separate construction sequences. Three brick arched doorways provide access on both the lower and
upper levels of the south wall of this room (Figure 51). Although the 1839 claim described the sugar house as 12 feet high, implying a single-story structure, it is clear
that the loading room was a two-story segment. It is quite possible that the purgeries and boiling house were 1½ stories with accessible attics.

Two purgeries flank the loading room (Figures 47 and 52). Each is separated
along the east-west axis into two coquina-lined cisterns or vats approximately 12
feet wide and 2 feet deep. It is possible that these cisterns were lead lined (Sitterson
1953:144). Although most of the outer walls of the purgeries are missing, it appears
that five segmentally arched windows were evenly spaced along the south wall of
each purgery, with three similar openings on the east and west end walls. A single
opening was located at the center of the north walls. The doors on the upper floor
of the storage room may have had hoists to facilitate the movement of barrels from
the purgeries to the upper storage level.

Spring House. The spring house, located west of the sugar works, consists of
partially subsurface rectangular coquina-block walls. It probably once had a wood
shingle roof on the 16-inch-thick walls. There is a series of 12-inch-wide openings

52. East purgery of Bulow sugar works.

regularly spaced about 3 feet below the present wall tops (Figure 53). The spring house now seasonally contains water and may have been used for cold storage.

Bulow Summary. In summary, the Bulow sugar works is an excellent example of the T-shaped sugar works, with the engine in a separate structure, the crusher probably between the engine house and boiling house, the sugar train and clarifier in the leg of the T, and the two purgeries in the arms. The upper level may have provided storage space for barrels.

Macrae

The Macrae sugar works site is located on the former Addison or "Carrickfergus" plantation in the southern part of the Tomoka State Park (Figure 1). The sugar works is located in a heavily wooded area that is accessible via a poorly maintained dirt road that begins at a locked gate within the adjacent development. Due to the access difficulties, it is presently not open to visitors.

All of the archaeology that has been conducted at the Addison-Macrae site has focused on the nearby Addison Blockhouse and adjacent house ruins. Archaeologist John W. Griffin (1952c) tested the Addison Blockhouse site in 1950 and completed drawings of the remains. More recently, archaeologist Ted Payne (personal

53. Bulow spring house.

communication 2001) has identified the probable location of the slave settlement associated with this site. In 2004, additional research and a historic structure report were completed on the Addison Blockhouse (Parks and Younkin 2004). Research on the sugar works has been much more limited. Herschel Shepard's graduate seminar in historic preservation at the University of Florida College of Design, Construction and Planning completed measured drawings of the Macrae sugar works (Shepard et al. 2000). These drawings were updated for the 2001 stabilization plan completed by SouthArc, Inc. (Wayne et al. 2001).

History of Addison–Macrae

During the British Period, the 2,000-acre John Moultrie grant included part of what would later become the Addison-Macrae holdings (Parks and Younkin 2004: 1–3). In 1816, John Addison, formerly a Bahamian planter and merchant, applied for a title to 1,414 acres on the Tomoka River. One of the witnesses to his application, fellow planter Joseph M. Hernandez, "testified that Addison had lived on the property, cleared substantial acreage, erected buildings for a great number of both whites and blacks and kept the land in well-ordered condition" (Stanton 1942). The royal surveyor (and owner of nearby property), Robert McHardy, stated that Addison's land "is very well organized with many slaves, stock buildings, fences, and all else that is found on a good plantation" (Strickland 1963:13). McHardy's map shows Addison's house and a group of 14 smaller structures to the south, possibly slave cabins (Payne and Griffin 2001:71).

Carrickfergus. Addison named his new plantation "Carrickfergus" (sometimes listed as "Currick Fergus") after his birthplace in Ireland. Although Addison had been a planter and merchant in the Bahamas (Cardwell 1976:19), and thus may have been familiar with Caribbean sugar works, his primary crop was cotton. He built a gin at Carrickfergus and produced $3,500 in cotton in 1823 (Bishop 1975:8). However, he also grew indigo, rice, produce, and some sugar, as well as raising live-stock. He had 67 slaves on the property, who were described as working the plan-tation "without 'beast or machinery'" (Stanton 1949).

Addison died in 1825, weeks after his grant was confirmed. The Carrickfer-gus property was inherited by his brother Thomas, who also died soon afterward. Both Addisons were buried on the Carrickfergus property (Stanton 1949). Prior to his death, Thomas Addison sold the plantation and slaves to his neighbor, Col. Thomas Dummett, for $24,000. By 1826, possibly due to his investment in the construction of a sugar works, Dummett was forced to mortgage the Carrickfer-gus property to Duncan and Kenneth Macrae (Bishop 1975:8; Schene 1976:31–32).

Macrae. In 1828, Carrickfergus and 24 slaves were acquired for $12,500 by the Macrae brothers, who turned the property into a sugar plantation (Schene 1976: 31–32). Kenneth Macrae died about 1830, but Duncan continued to operate the property, eventually doubling the number of slaves and becoming one of the larg-est slave owners in the county (Schene 1976:33).

Presumably, the Macraes occupied the old Addison house, which should have still been in reasonably good condition due to the short period between Addison's death and the Macrae purchase. Foundations for a house, the remains of what was probably originally the kitchen, and a coquina-lined well are located 250 feet from the sugar works. The house remains consist of a 15- by 30-foot coquina founda-tion with a chimney at the north end. Tabby surfacing for piazzas is present on the other three sides of the foundation. The building appears to have been frame con-struction, possibly only a single story in height. The detached kitchen, now known as the Addison Blockhouse, has been extensively altered over the years. It seems to have originally been a small coquina building about 11½ by 15 feet in size with a massive hearth and cistern on the north wall (Griffin 1952c:276). During a recent visit to the site, this author noted that the feature identified as a cistern could alter-natively have been a bake oven.

Based on a date once carved on a block above the sugar works door, Duncan Macrae built the sugar works in 1832 (Stanton 1949; Hunter 1934). At 135 feet long, the Macrae sugar works is actually longer than Bulow's; but overall the square foot-age is probably somewhat less, as Macrae has a single purgery.

This was not the best time to start sugar production. A severe freeze hurt the cane crop in 1835 (Cardwell 1976:20), and at the end of that same year, only three years after the sugar works was built, the Second Seminole War began, forcing occupants to abandon the plantations. After Bulowville burned in late January 1836, the Carolina Regiment of Volunteers moved south into the Tomoka River area. Troops from this regiment occupied both Carrickfergus and the nearby destroyed Dummett sugar works (Kipp 1967:2E; Griffin 1951:19). The occupying troops reported that at Carrickfergus "The dwelling house, sugar house and every other building on the place except those two mentioned [a fowl house and a Negro shack] were destroyed" (Smith 1836:196). Research by archaeologist John Griffin (1951:19) demonstrated that the troops rebuilt the ruined Carrickfergus kitchen and adjacent round cistern located approximately 250 feet from the sugar works into a small storehouse with a watchtower, surrounded by a breastwork and the deep trenches reported in the archival records (Cohen 1964:148).

On March 10, 1836, the Seminoles attacked the encampment, but withdrew when they decided the soldiers were prepared to counterattack. A report of the attack stated that the Seminoles hid in the ruins of the sugar works approximately 200 yards from the army's tents (Cohen 1964:151–153). Another account stated that the access road ran by the sugar works to the encampment at the Carrickfergus house (Smith 1836:198). By the end of March, "Camp M'Rae" was abandoned, although a stockade reportedly remained to shelter 75 to 85 soldiers too sick to travel. After three months, the remaining soldiers were removed and the camp ceased to exist (Cardwell 1976:21).

Post–Seminole War. The Macrae plantation was not reestablished after the Second Seminole War, and the author assumes that the property remained basically undeveloped until it was acquired by the park. The Addison Blockhouse was "restored" during the early twentieth century with the probable addition of the existing watchtower and crenelations along the tops of the walls (Griffin 1952c:276, 278). Tomoka State Park now owns all of the Addison-Macrae structures and works hard to maintain them with limited funding. The sugar works description below is based on the 2001 study (Wayne et al. 2001).

Macrae Sugar Works

The remains of the Macrae sugar works primarily consist of the sugar works themselves (Figure 54). However, there are nearby piles of coquina rubble that suggest the presence of other structures, possibly including dwellings for the overseer or sugar striker. A second probable coquina chimney fall is located somewhat further to the west of the sugar house.

Sugar House. The sugar house is basically an L-shaped building with the boiling train and engine house in the long leg of the L and the purgery in the shorter leg (Figure 55). Only the northeast corner walls remain standing, and it is unclear

54. Looking southwest at Macrae sugar works.

whether foundations extend from the remaining legs to form enclosed rectangles. The 2001 study (Wayne et al. 2001:128) speculated that the purgery and engine house may have been enclosed under gable roofing, while the boiling house was open on the west side with either a shed roof stretching between the two gabled sections or a cross gable roof connecting the other sections.

The remaining walls of the Macrae sugar works are very well-constructed random ashlar coquina on both interior and exterior (Figure 54). The walls have coquina blocks on the interior and exterior, with rubble infill between the outer walls, resulting in a total wall thickness of approximately 17 inches. There are traces of lime or tabby plaster on the exterior walls. Where the walls are intact and retain their 4-inch-deep capstone, they reach a height of about 10 feet, indicating a single-story building.

The extant walls have five windows and a door on the east side, with one window and a probable door edge on the north side. The windows are beveled inward, with plaster extending into the window openings. Fragments of coquina block on the interior side of the sills served as stops for wooden shutters.

The Macrae engine house is at the far (south) end of the long leg of the L, sharing a chimney with the boiling train (Figure 55). A series of masonry half walls supported the engine and boiler in the interior of this room (Figure 56). The outer walls have no visible footing. The east wall seems to be built of small pieces of coquina rubble mortared together. A cold joint between the support walls and the east wall indicates that the support walls were not built until the machinery was on site, in order to space them for an exact fit.

MACRAE SUGAR MILL, 8Vo193
TOMOKA BASIN GEOPARK

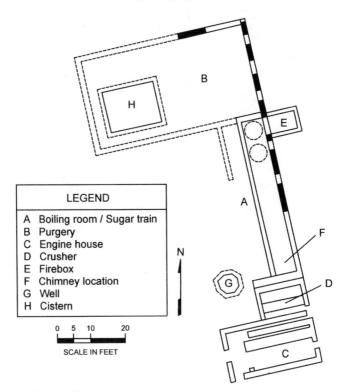

55. Plan of Macrae sugar works.

There is a probable stoking hole for the engine at the end of the boiler area in the southeast corner of the building (Figure 55). A short wall on the west side of the engine house encloses the engine firebox area. Notches in the walls were probably for supports for the boiler and engine. An opening at the west end of the south wall provided access to the equipment, as did a second opening in the west wall. There is no evidence of plaster on the walls within the engine house—probably because the machinery would have hidden the interior walls. Another cold joint between the west wall and the north wall of the engine house indicates that this segment of wall was built after the flywheel was put in place.

The crusher was located to the north of the engine (Figure 55). Gaps beneath the walls between the flywheel and crusher suggest that a flue from the boiler ran beneath the equipment to the chimney located north of the crusher. Both flywheel area and crusher have vertical notches in the walls for supports for the equipment. Back-to-back walls with a cold joint mark the junction of the crusher and the boiling house.

56. Macrae engine/boiler/crusher area.

The east wall of the sugar works has collapsed in the area between the crusher and sugar train where the chimney was located (Figure 55). A large pile of coquina block, brick, and earth extends on both the interior and exterior of the structure at this point, marking the collapsed chimney.

The sugar train seems to closely resemble that of Bulow, with a platform for a clarifier at the south end adjacent to the chimney and five kettles extending to the north (Figures 55 and 57). The train is built of coquina, brick, and firebrick, tapering to the north; some of the bricks are shaped to fit the kettles. A four-inch-wide ledge on the west side of the train supported a platform for the workers about three feet below the kettle rims.

The firebox for the train is located on the exterior of the east wall at the north end of the train (Figures 55 and 58). The east wall of the sugar works above the stoking hole once had a stone arch with the surrounding coquina shaped to fit the curve. The exposed wall fill in the missing arch contains small brick fragments as well as coquina rubble. The wall beneath the arch is recessed 10 inches and plastered with lime plaster. The stoking hole beneath the arch is constructed of corbeled coquina blocks in a smaller arch with a larger block serving as a lintel. The roughness of the masonry suggests that an iron flue like that found at Three Chimneys may have been present.

Two other openings are located at the base of the east wall near the south end of the train. The openings are roughly centered on the windows above them, and

57. Looking southeast at Macrae sugar train.

58. Firebox of Macrae sugar train.

59. Macrae sugar works octagonal well.

were probably supplemental stoking points for the train. Similar openings are present at both Cruger-DePeyster and Dunlawton.

A large coquina-block well is located adjacent to the south end of the sugar train (Figure 55). The blocks in this well have been shaped to form an octagonal interior (Figure 59). Grooving on the blocks indicates the location of vertical support beams for the windlass.

Cooling Area and Purgery. The area at the north end of the sugar train (Figure 55) probably served as the cooling area, and for general movement of sugar between the train and the purgery. The junction of the purgery and boiling house is marked by another cold joint. The purgery itself is defined by a footing of large square coquina blocks on three sides of the purgery (Figure 60). Due to the missing facing of the interior walls of the purgery, it could not be determined if it was plastered. A cistern is located in the southwest corner of the purgery (Figures 55 and 60). The cistern has a coquina outer wall lined with half-bricks in a rowlock pattern; the bricks were then plastered. The hard bottom indicates a similar brick and plaster lining under the accumulated detritus.

Although the cistern seems rather small for the overall size of the boiling house and purgery (cf. Bulow, Cruger-DePeyster, and Dunlawton), it may have functioned like an example shown in Cleland's 1836 description of the proper sugar works (Figure 14) and like those described by Spalding in 1816. In those cases, a

60. Looking east at purgery and cistern of Macrae sugar works.

fairly small cistern is fed by slanting wooden flooring, which forms a funnel from a raised floor holding the draining barrels.

Macrae Summary. To summarize, the linear arrangement of Macrae—with the engine, crusher, and sugar train in a single line with a shared chimney—was probably designed to promote efficiency, as was the location of all parts of the process in a single building. It is very similar to Olcott's 1857 plan of an idealized sugar works (Figure 6). But the small area allotted to the crusher seems to be rather restrictive for that activity. The small purgery cistern is also an unusual design for this area, although it is consistent with Cleland's 1836 and Spalding's 1816 guidelines for sugar making (see Figure 14). The cold joints between the different parts of the building seem to indicate a sequence of construction periods, as does the variation in the masonry itself (lack of footings in the boiling house and use of small coquina pieces in the engine house). Overall, however, Macrae reflects not only a design that indicates extensive knowledge of sugar making, but also high-quality masonry construction with attention to finish details such as stucco and the octagonal well.

Cruger-DePeyster

The Cruger-DePeyster sugar works is located on the outskirts of New Smyrna Beach at 1050 Old Mission Road (Figure 1), and is often referred to as the New

Smyrna Sugar Mill. Presently, the sugar works is the centerpiece of a state-owned park managed by Volusia County. The park is open from 8 a.m. to sunset. See www.newsmyrnabeach.com/resources/historic-ruins.html for more information. Volusia County has recently installed excellent interpretative signage at the site.

In the early years of the twentieth century, the sugar works was erroneously identified as the seventeenth-century Spanish "Mission of Atocuimi de Jororo" (Historic American Building Survey 1934). The research of journalist Charles H. Coe and archaeologist John W. Griffin successfully proved that the building did not even exist during the First Spanish Period, but rather was a sugar works built in the Territorial Period (Coe 1941). The site was recorded for the Historic American Building Survey (HABS) in 1934 as a mission/sugar works and listed on the National Register of Historic Places in 1970.

The most extensive recent study of the Cruger-DePeyster sugar works was completed in 1994 by Environmental Services, Inc. (Smith et al. 1994). This study included archaeological testing, an evaluation of the structural remains, and preservation recommendations. In 2000, limited excavations were conducted adjacent to the engine house in preparation for stabilization of the walls in this area (Piatek 2000). The 2001 stabilization plan by SouthArc, Inc., completed measured drawings of the ruins (Wayne et al. 2001).

Coe (1941:12) wrote of this site: "A first view of the ruins rarely fails to impress the thoughtful beholder with its great size and the large sum of money and months of labor that evidently were expended in its construction and equipment." Cruger-DePeyster is very similar to Bulow in layout and architectural details, and was probably heavily influenced by the older mill. The primary difference is that Cruger-DePeyster has a single purgery, resulting in an L shape rather than a T. As at Bulow and Macrae, there is no indication of experimentation at the Cruger-DePeyster site. Either the builders knew what they were doing, or they closely followed the examples of the existing sugar works in the region.

History of Cruger-DePeyster

The area of the Cruger-DePeyster sugar works was originally part of Andrew Turnbull's failed New Smyrna colony established in 1768 and abandoned in 1777. In 1801, during the Second Spanish Period, a portion of the Turnbull property was granted to Ambrose Hull. Hull built a house at the present Old Fort Park tract in New Smyrna Beach; this house was destroyed during the Patriot War of 1812 (Historic Property Associates, Inc. [HPA] 1988:14).

Cruger-DePeyster Ownership. After Hull died in 1821, his property was divided and sold (HPA 1988:14). Two New Yorkers, Henry Cruger and William DePeyster, bought 600 acres of the Hull property, which included the area of the present sugar works (Smith et al. 1994:22).

Cruger and DePeyster focused on developing the property as a sugar plantation. They borrowed $10,000 from William Kemble to buy machinery from the West Point Foundry Company of New York. This machinery was to include a complete sawmill, steam engines, and a sugar mill (Bathe 1955:109). Kemble was also to act as agent for the two owners. In return for his loan, Kemble was given a $5,000 mortgage and a promise of repayment plus interest by 1832 (Bathe 1955:109). Unfortunately this promise was not kept. In 1833, Cruger and DePeyster borrowed an additional $4,000 from Joseph and Charles Lawton to make a token payment to Kemble in order to continue operating the sugar works (Bathe 1955:111).

During the few years that the sugar works operated, the plantation's overseer, John Sheldon, reportedly lived in a frame house at the site of Ambrose Hull's home at Old Fort Park. Cruger and DePeyster were basically absentee owners who provided a house for the manager, rather than building one for themselves (Griffin 1993). No information is available on the location of the slave cabins that were undoubtedly part of this operation.

Only three years after the partners began construction of the sugar works, the facility was destroyed by the Seminole on December 28, 1835, along with the rest of New Smyrna (HPA 1988:22) (Figure 61). By the time the Seminole destroyed the mill, Cruger and DePeyster were in worse financial straits. The Lawton brothers sued Cruger and DePeyster in 1834 and again in 1839 in an attempt to recover their loan (Smith et al. 1994:24). Then in 1845, William Kemble also sued DePeyster, after Cruger's death and the destruction of the mill, to recoup his original loan. As a part of this suit, Kemble petitioned for sale of the property to erase a debt of $8,316.56 (Bathe 1955:111). Kemble, the only bidder, acquired the property for $4,050, including the "steam engines, machinery, utensils and fixtures in each and every of said mills belonging and appertaining and also the negro slaves" (Bathe 1955:111). It is important to note that Kemble referred to "engines," suggesting that there were separate engines for the sugar works and sawmill (Herschel E. Shepard Jr., architect, personal communication 2008). Kemble promptly sold the machinery from the mill to John J. Marshall, who was then rebuilding the destroyed Dunlawton sugar works in nearby Port Orange (St. Johns County Court Records 1846; Bathe 1955:111).

Connor Ownership and Mission Myth. The sugar works was never reestablished, and by the 1890s the property encompassing the ruins was owned by Isadora Matthews. In 1893, New York stockbroker Washington E. Connor purchased the 10-acre sugar works property for $400 as a birthday present for his wife, Jeanette Thurber Connor. Mrs. Connor was supposedly an authority on the early Spanish history of Florida (Smith et al. 1994:26). Her husband felt that the arched windows of the sugar works ruins were too elaborate for a factory; therefore, he believed it must have been built earlier for another purpose (Smith et al. 1994:26). Mrs. Connor proceeded to promote the idea that this was a Franciscan mission established in 1696 for the Jororo Indians.

61. *The Ruins of the Sugar House,* by John Rogers Vinton, 1843. (Courtesy of the Sam and Robbie Vickers Florida Collection)

It should be noted that Mrs. Connor was involved in similar moves in southeast Georgia to identify tabby sugar works in that area as missions. Marmaduke Floyd, who helped debunk the mission theory in Georgia, felt that the drive to identify these masonry ruins as missions was an outgrowth of the publicity given to the masonry California missions after World War I, and the subsequent popularity of Mission-style architecture. He believed that real estate agents attempting to attract buyers to new subdivisions in Florida and Georgia seized on the mission myth to promote sales (Floyd 1937:4–5).

Mrs. Connor gave talks supporting her view, and the Connors even installed a bronze plaque in 1926 that identified the ruins as a Franciscan mission to the Jororo Indians (Strickland 1985:43). The Connors were instrumental in getting the site recorded by the Historic American Building Survey (HABS) as a mission. In 1929, they deeded the property to the Florida State Park Service, which remains the owner today (Southeast Volusia Chamber of Commerce 1997).

The Connors' claim inspired Charles Coe, editor of the *Florida Star* newspaper, to write a 32-page pamphlet debunking this theory (Coe 1941). Coe also attacked claims that brass candlestick fragments found at the site were associated with the mission (Coe 1941:21–22). Archaeologist John W. Griffin had the candlesticks identified by Colonial Williamsburg and the Metropolitan Museum of Art, both of whom dated them as nineteenth-century English (Griffin 1993). Griffin also measured the sugar works and determined that it was built using English measurements, and that these measurements corresponded almost exactly to those of Bulow (Coe 1941:13, 16–17; Strickland 1985:43; Davidson 1950b:23). In fact, in comparing the two sites, he stated that "The machinery rooms (where the steam boiler and the cane grinding machinery was installed) are placed identically and measure exactly the same size. . . . The same is true of the size and location of the boiling kettle area. The crystallizing vats are also identically located as are the chimneys. Overall length is nearly the same" (Davidson 1950b:23). Griffin (1993) speculated, based on the similarities in the surfaces, that some of the blocks in the sugar works had been scavenged from the foundation at Old Fort Park, which was part of the same property at that time.

There are also the written records documenting Cruger and DePeyster's purchases, as well as a Catholic church study that documented that there were no missions south of St. Augustine (Gannon 1965:64). Both add to the evidence supporting the site as a nineteenth-century sugar works, not a mission.

Cruger–DePeyster Sugar Works

The Cruger-DePeyster sugar works consists of an L-shaped building containing the boiling house and purgery and a separate building for the engine (Figures 62 and 63). As previously noted, the plan is very similar to Bulow except that there is only one purgery (compare to Figure 47). However, as Coe (1941:12–13) has noted, the construction quality is not as good, particularly in the masonry, where courses of stone do not have sufficient overlap, resulting in joints lining up and subsequently failing. The blocks vary in size with small fragments of both block and bricks used as infill. There were apparently early problems with the stability of the arches as evidenced by the presence of iron lintels at the boiling house and purgery doors. Coe (1941:12–13) noted an iron tie rod near the top of the east wall of the engine house, the wall with three arched windows. At the present time, the south and east walls of the purgery, the north wall of the boiling house, and the south and east walls of the engine house are the only standing walls (Figure 62). Foundations are identifiable for the balance of the engine house, boiling house, and purgery. Coe (1941:12–13) speculated that there was also a shed on the west side of the engine house (Figure 63).

According to one account, the Cruger-DePeyster sugar works had a steam engine with two boilers which was rated at "30 nominal horse power" (Bathe 1955:115). Coe (1941:12–13) described the 10-foot-long iron walking beam near the engine house as the only thing left of the engine. Architect Herschel Shepard, like Bathe, believes that the walking beam at Cruger-DePeyster was for the sawmill (Herschel E. Shepard Jr., personal communication 2008). Just as at the Bulow sugar works, it is probable that the sawmill was operated by a separate engine that shared the two boilers. As previously noted, Kemble referred to "engines" when describing the property (Bathe 1955:111). Shepard notes that the engine remains

62. Looking north at Cruger-DePeyster sugar works.

at Dunlawton, which were originally from Cruger-DePeyster, show no evidence of attachments that might run equipment other than the crusher (Herschel E. Shepard Jr., personal communication 2008). It should be noted, however, that a sugar mill built in 1861 by West Point Foundry for Hacienda la Esperanza in Puerto Rico does use a walking beam in the engine (Wills 2009:21). Thus it is possible that due to the incomplete nature of the equipment at Dunlawton, this walking beam could have been part of the original mill engine.

Limited archaeological testing completed in 1994 and 2000 indicated that no builders trenches were used for construction of the sugar works (Smith et al. 1994:88; Piatek 2000:3). The first testing included an excavation adjacent to the chimney base and north wall of the boiling house. The lowest level of this wall was placed directly on the natural ground surface. Rather than level the blocks at their bases, the tops were leveled, covered with a layer of shell mortar and "a long, wide coquina block" (Smith et al. 1994:41). The later excavations were placed on the exterior of the engine house at the southwest corner, midway on the east wall and at the northeast corner. These units also failed to identify a construction trench, although the author speculated that there could be a trench on the interior of the walls, or that the trench was dug only the width of the wall itself (Piatek 2000:3).

The following description is based largely on the fieldwork completed in 2001 (Wayne et al. 2001). As at Bulow, concrete sidewalks and low chains lead visitors through the site and deter access to the ruins (Figure 62).

Engine House. The engine house is a separate building from the rest of the sugar

CRUGER-DEPEYSTER, 8Vo184
NEW SMYRNA BEACH, FLORIDA

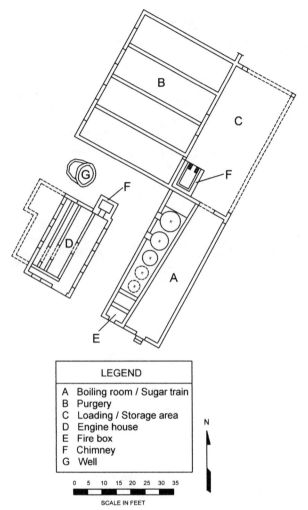

LEGEND

A Boiling room / Sugar train
B Purgery
C Loading / Storage area
D Engine house
E Fire box
F Chimney
G Well

N

0 5 10 15 20 25 30 35
SCALE IN FEET

63. Plan of Cruger-DePeyster sugar works.

works, just as it is at Bulow. Coe (1941:13) noted that the construction was the same as the other building but "Perhaps it is a little more finished, as this building, with its costly machinery, was the most valuable part of the Sugar-Mill, and probably was the first to be built."

An oval well is located between the purgery and the engine house (Figure 63). The coquina-lined structure appears to be dry-laid with 14-inch-thick walls; the west side has brick repairs.

64. Looking east at Cruger-DePeyster engine house.

The chimney for the engine house steps in at about eight feet above present grade and then again eight feet above that step (Figure 64). There is a cold joint between the chimney and the north wall of the engine house. The flue on the south side is brick lined. Openings in the north wall and interior walls indicate the locations of the boiler, flywheel, and engines (Figure 65).

The east wall has an interior ledge at ground level, presumably to support equipment. The portion of the wall below the window sills is very rough unfinished small stones with undressed mortar, probably because it would have been hidden by the machinery. From the sills to the top of the wall, the stones are dressed and the mortar is tooled. Tall, graceful arched window openings are located at intervals along this wall (Figures 62 and 64). Based on a fragmentary wall, there was a similar arched opening on the north wall adjacent to the chimney at the same spacing as those on the east wall. On the interior of the east wall, there is a second ledge above the arches that is missing the interior face (Figure 64). This is the area in which Coe (1941:12–13) described an iron rod, which is visible in an early photograph of the building. The presence of an iron tie rod and an iron lintel in the southern window suggests that failure of the masonry occurred early in the life of the building.

The south wall of the entry antechamber has another arched window with a sill lower than those on the east wall (Figure 64). The six-foot-wide door on the south wall is topped by an arch that has been rebuilt.

65. Looking southwest at Cruger-DePeyster engine house and well.

A depressed area of rubble on the west side of the engine house may indicate the other room or shed suggested by Coe's (1941:13) descriptions and the HABS (1934) drawings. The large iron walking beam now on display was found in this area. A pit to the west of the engine house appears to be lined with stone and is presumably also associated with the sugar works, although its function is unknown. Presumably the crusher was located between the engine house and the boiling house, as at Bulow.

Boiling Room. The boiling room walls are missing, although foundations are identifiable on all sides (Figures 62, 63, and 66). The HABS (1934) drawings indicate that there was a flagstone floor identifiable in the northeast corner of this room. A partial arch remains at the northeast corner, indicating that the walls probably had arched openings like those in the engine house. Coe's (1941:12–13) description of seven well-preserved arched windows indicates that at least three remained in the boiling house when he saw it. He noted that "There probably were as many more, at least, in the absent walls, as light and ventilation were absolutely necessary in a sugar-mill. None of them are nor ever were glazed" (Coe 1941:12–13). As at Macrae and Bulow, the windows would have been shuttered.

The sugar train tapers on the east side to the firebox on the south end (Figure 63). No brick is visible in the kettle row, which is missing much of its upper construction. It was a five-kettle train with a platform for the clarifier at the north

66. Looking northeast at Cruger-DePeyster boiling room.

end next to the chimney and a firebox at the south (cf. Bulow). Three kettles remain on the surface of the train, although it is not known if they are original to the site. Two 15-inch-wide openings, possibly flues, are present in the west wall at the approximate location of the two largest kettles—just as they were at Macrae. The west side of the boiling room would have been the cooling area.

The firebox at the south end of the train is the most intact of the fireboxes at any of the sugar works studied, except those at Dunlawton. At Cruger-DePeyster, it is separated from the train by an iron lintel, which is essentially a rectangular tube about eight feet long with walls about one inch thick (Figure 66). Based on notches in the stone walls of the firebox, a second iron bar the same size was located south of the existing bar.

Storage/Loading Area. The base of the largely missing chimney for the sugar train has cold joints with the adjacent walls. A brick-lined flue is located on the north side (Figure 67), with the bricks extending into the center of the chimney base. Probing revealed a coquina floor and a thin stucco coating on the chimney interior. A 15-inch square opening with an unknown function is located in the west wall adjacent to the chimney. Based on the construction of the walls behind the chimney, it stepped in and tapered like the chimney of the engine house. The areas that would be hidden by the chimney are built of coquina rubble with tabby mortar.

Although there is a fragmentary wall at the northeast end of the north boiling room wall and at the northeast corner of the purgery, probing in 2001 did not

67. Looking southwest at chimney area of Cruger-DePeyster sugar works.

identify any foundation remains to close the space between the boiling room and purgery. Investigations by John Griffin in 1950 also failed to locate a foundation in this area, so it may have been an open space (Davidson 1950b:23).

The arched doorways opening to the boiling room and purgery are the doorways that have the iron lintels described by Coe. The original lintel in the boiling room door arch hooked back into the coquina, suggesting it was placed when the building was erected. This arch has recently been repaired, and the lintel is no longer visible. The arch to the purgery is a flat arch, which would have required a lintel when it was built; the present arch has twentieth-century repairs. The foundation wall is exposed as a sill in this doorway.

The west wall of the handling area is constructed of random ashlar coquina with large blocks in a rusticated pattern around the openings. The balance of the wall consists of relatively small stones with tight joints and an abundance of coquina chinking. There are at least two layers of stone in the wall.

Purgery. The south wall of the purgery has no openings (Figure 68). The lower courses of this wall consist of large, long blocks topped by approximately six feet of small, irregular blocks, and then completed by large, regular-cut blocks. Due to insufficient overlap of the stones, severe cracking occurred in this wall. The wall has a 24-inch-wide footing, which projects about 3 inches; the wall itself is 16 inches thick.

Only the south end of the west purgery wall is present; the north wall is completely missing (Figure 68). The interior of the purgery is divided by three east-

68. Looking southwest at purgery of Cruger-DePeyster.

west foundations into four equal chambers about six inches deep (Figures 63 and 68). Previous testing in this area exposed what appears to be a stucco floor (Smith et al. 1994:32), and yellowish stucco is visible on the foundation of the east wall.

Cruger-DePeyster Summary. Although the workmanship and materials of the Cruger-DePeyster sugar works are not comparable in quality to those of Bulow, the design clearly draws either from Bulow or from similar sugar works in the Caribbean. The graceful arches of the engine house were probably duplicated in the boiling house and possibly the purgery. While arches are a good structural means of putting an opening in a masonry building, the regular placement and graceful dimensions of these arches suggest that the builders also wanted to impress visitors with the architectural style and sophistication of the structure—as well as the expense invested in its construction.

Dunlawton

The Dunlawton sugar works is located in Sugar Mill Botanical Gardens on Old Sugar Mill Road in Port Orange (Figure 1). The gardens are open from dawn to dusk daily. The property is owned by Volusia County but is leased to the Botanical Gardens of Volusia, Inc. (www.dunlawtonsugarmillgardens.org). The remains of the sugar works lie at one corner of the gardens immediately adjacent to Old Mill Road. Plans are under way to provide limited access and additional interpretation for the site. In addition to the remains of the Dunlawton sugar works, an animal-powered cane grinder from the Samuel Williams sugar works once located in Daytona Beach is on display in another part of the gardens (Figure 8).

The Dunlawton sugar works was first documented in 1955 by St. Augustine engineer Greville Bathe. Bathe compiled a history of the property and drew plans of the building remains (Bathe 1955). In 1973, Dunlawton was listed on the National Register of Historic Places. A number of studies and restoration efforts have been completed at the site dating back to the late 1970s. In 1977, Herschel Shepard Jr., of Fisher & Shepard, Architects & Planners, Inc., completed a structural analysis and preservation plan for the site. This document included measured drawings of the extant machinery (Shepard 1977). The following year, Curtiss Peterson (1978) provided an evaluation of the extant machinery with additional preservation recommendations. Eventually, recommendations from both of these documents were implemented, including restoration of the engine and cane crusher in 1979 to 1980 (Wayne et al. 1991:48). Additional restoration of the boiling house was implemented in 1998 (Piatek 1998). Archaeological testing was completed in the engine house prior to its restoration (Stewart 1979). SouthArc, Inc., completed an archaeological survey of the gardens in 1991, including limited excavations at the sugar works and a reevaluation by Shepard of the ruins' condition (Wayne et al. 1991). Additional testing was completed by archaeologist Bruce Piatek (1998) in conjunction with the 1998 restoration efforts. As this book was being finished, further protection efforts were under way.

During the 1979 to 1980 restoration, the crusher was completely dismantled and the original heart cedar wood supports were replaced with pressure-treated pine with the same mortise-and-tenon construction. The crusher was reattached to the repaired masonry base. When the machinery was measured and reinstalled, great care was taken to place the parts in their proper relationships in the hope that the equipment could eventually be restored to operating condition provided it could be moved by a power source other than steam. At a later date, the wood beams were again replaced, but the current reinstallation does not allow for the possibility of running the machinery. All of the metal items, including the machinery, were also painted black during the most recent repairs (Herschel E. Shepard Jr., architect, personal communication 2008).

Dunlawton is the only one of the four fully developed sugar works that has any indication of adaptation in its construction. This is a result of the comparatively lengthy period in which it was used, and the fact that it is the only East Florida sugar works rebuilt after the Second Seminole War.

History of Dunlawton

Like the Cruger-DePeyster site, Dunlawton was once part of the Turnbull Grant, which was abandoned in 1777 (Bathe 1955:104). The next record of the property dates to 1804, when Patrick Dean, a merchant from the Bahamas, and his uncle, John Bunch, a planter, acquired portions of the Turnbull grant. Dean acquired the 995 acres that would become Dunlawton, while Bunch's acreage was immediately to the north (Wilson 1957:17). Dean and Bunch had apparently acquired significant debts in the Bahamas, and saw Florida as a means of recouping their fortunes. Although Bunch's wife, Cecily, was a member of a wealthy family, she sold most of her holdings in order to acquire additional slaves, since land grants in Florida at that time were based on head rights (i.e., the number of occupants) (Works Progress Administration 1940:244–245).

Although the plantations were temporarily abandoned during the Patriot War, by 1816 to 1817 Dean was producing both indigo and sugar on the property (Cardwell 2006:3–4). Bathe (1955:105) says Dean erected "a stone mill worked by animal power" to grind his cane. However, in 1818 Patrick Dean was killed by an Indian; he left his plantation to his aunt, Cecily Bunch (Cardwell 2006:4). Within a year the property was described by John Addison as abandoned, with only a chimney remaining of the well-constructed house (Addison 1819:376). Cecily Bunch apparently died not long after Dean, specifying in her will that the former Dean plantation should go to the Bunches' grandson at John Bunch's death (Reeves ca. 1979). John Bunch continued to operate the two properties as a single plantation until 1830, producing both cotton and sugar on the Dean acreage (Reeves ca. 1979).

In 1830, as specified in Cecily Bunch's will but prior to his death, John Bunch gave the Dean acreage to his grandson, John Bonnemaison Bunch McHardy. McHardy was a highly successful British naval officer (he ultimately became an admiral) who had no interest in operating a Florida plantation. He promptly sold the property to Joseph and Charles Lawton of Charleston for $3,000. The Lawtons were land agents, attorneys, bankers, and merchants who bought and sold plantations, slaves, and crops throughout the area (Cardwell 2006:5). The name Dunlawton presumably dates to the Lawton ownership, as Dunn was Lawton's mother's maiden name (Burns 1988:7).

Anderson Ownership. In 1832, the Lawtons sold the plantation to Sarah Perry Anderson for $4,500 (Fitzgerald 1939:13). Mrs. Anderson and her two sons were previously residents of the Tomoka area, and moved to the Mosquito (Halifax) River area in anticipation of gaining better land (Bathe 1955:107). They hired John R. Mitchell and Thomas H. Hall to build structures to replace the deteriorated Dean buildings. This work included a dwelling, overseer's house, kitchen, corn house, landing, boathouse, lumber house, workshop, flat house, 21 slave cabins, and coquina sugar works. The mill's machinery was installed by Scottish engineer John McMurchie, who listed an eight-horsepower engine, a mill, kettles, clarifiers, connecting machinery, ladles, and other tools, plus installation for a sum of $4,850 (McMurchie 1836). It should be noted that in McMurchie's deposition for Anderson's post–Seminole War claims, he stated "that with a few exceptions he erected all the Engines used in East Florida" (McMurchie 1836). Thus he is another candidate as the Scottish engineer at Bulow and Spring Garden.

One contemporary description of the Anderson property remains. According to this anonymous and undated observation, the "Anderson Brothers built a mill of two separate rooms with walls of coquina. The machine room has four windows and the engine to turn the wheels that crush the cane and a part of the pipe to carry the juice. The adjoining room has 10 boiling vats under these juice boxes. After cooking the juice runs through a concrete trough. The cane is carried from the stacks to the crusher by means of a working chain 75 feet long which has board slats fastened to it [see Figure 9]. The mass of machinery is supported on timbers" (qtd. in Bathe 1955:108).

Within four years, the property was in ruins as a result of the Second Seminole War. Dunlawton became the site of two skirmishes during the war. On January 18, 1836, the Mosquito Roarers under the leadership of Maj. Benjamin Putnam went to Dunlawton to determine its condition and retrieve any provisions that might remain. The troop of about 40 soldiers was attacked at the mill by a party of as many as 150 Seminole led by Coacoochee. The Mosquito Roarers took shelter in the mill ruins. When it appeared that the Indians were about to surround them, the troops retreated to their boats and returned to their fortifications at Bulow, leaving Dunlawton to the Seminole (Motte 1953:279; *Niles Weekly Register* 1836a:595).

The second very minor skirmish occurred in the fall of 1837. A slave named John Philip, who had belonged to the Seminole chief King Philip, agreed to lead the troops to an Indian camp south of the Tomoka River. A detachment of 170 men under the leadership of Gen. Joseph M. Hernandez moved south to the Dunlawton ruins where they bivouacked. Jacob Rhett Motte, a soldier under Hernandez's command, described it as "the blackened ruins of the Dunlawton Mill" (Motte 1953:119). About midnight the troops surrounded the nearby Indian encampment. The Seminoles had posted no guards and were taken by surprise, surrendering to Hernandez without a shot being fired. The captives included King Philip (Motte 1953:119–120).

After the war, the Andersons never attempted to restore the plantation, although they did file claims for $38,000 in damages (Cardwell 2006:20; Bathe 1955:108). Interestingly, this claim did not mention the sugar boiling house or steam-powered mill (Strickland 1985:40), although the McMurchie (1836) deposition provided costs for the equipment in the sugar works. The claim did list a dwelling, overseer's house, kitchen, corn house, 21 slave cabins, workshop, engine house (perhaps the sugar works?), boats, and lumber (Strickland 1985:37, 40). It is clear from the list that the owners lived in a modest 1½-story structure, as did their overseer, whose house was about half the size of the owner's dwelling. In fact, the corn house was listed as being as valuable ($150) as the overseer's house. Based on an average occupation of five slaves per dwelling, the Andersons may have had as many as 100 slaves at Dunlawton.

Post–Seminole War Ownership. In 1846, Mrs. Anderson sold Dunlawton to John J. Marshall, a carpenter and master builder from Charleston, South Carolina, for $8,000 (Cardwell 2006:23). Marshall rebuilt and expanded the mill, installing machinery he purchased from the destroyed Cruger-DePeyster mill in nearby New Smyrna Beach. By 1851, he was producing approximately 200 tons of sugar with 25 slaves (Bathe 1955:111). Unfortunately, falling prices in the sugar market led Marshall to abandon his efforts (Payne and Griffin 2001:96). The following year he sold the plantation to fellow Charlestonian William P. Vaux. However, Vaux, who was a live-oaker (one who harvested oaks for shipbuilding), apparently did not have the money to pay for the mill. He sold a partial interest to James and Samuel Ravenel of South Carolina. The deed notes that there was an "engine, sugar works, corn mills and buildings" along with "a Steam Saw Mill" (Vaux 1853). The money from the partial sale was evidently still insufficient to pay his debt, because the plantation reverted to Marshall in 1855 (Cardwell 2006:30).

By the time Marshall regained the plantation he had moved to Louisiana, leaving Dunlawton under the supervision of an overseer, Washington Sharpe. But Marshall apparently did not operate the plantation during this period (Cardwell 2006:30). One account indicates that the owner, or at least the resident, of Dunlawton during the Civil War was neither Marshall nor Sharpe, but a local fisherman and boatbuilder named Elijah F. McDonald, who lived in a log house on the property (Strickland 1985:40; Hebel 1955:9A). During the war, the plantation was reactivated to supply sugar and salt for the military. When sugar was not being processed, seawater was hauled in by barrels and boiled in the sugar trains to produce salt, a vital commodity to the army. Reportedly, the nearby large oak tree sheltered the soldiers encamped to await their cargoes (Bathe 1955:112).

William Daugherty bought Dunlawton in 1870, and his son Charles occupied the plantation. However, neither Daugherty was interested in planting, so it remained inactive (Fitzgerald 1939:13). Mathias Day of Ohio visited the property in 1870 and wrote a detailed description in his diary: "We found the Dunlawton Place of 450 acres well-drained, with heavy canals and smaller ditches; a large stone sugar house with two Jamaica trams; a large mill with rolls three feet and six inches by twenty-two inches; cane carriers, sundry tanks, purging house, cemented cisterns and a well in the middle of the boiling room; also two good chimney stacks, an engine about 60 horsepower, and two large old boilers. The sugar house is probably 160 by 50 feet" (qtd. in Bathe 1955:112–113).

An 1874 map shows the mill, with a house and possible tenant cabins located to the west of the present botanical gardens. The map also shows agricultural fields northeast and south of the mill, with open areas to the north, west, and southwest.

There were a number of drainage ditches cut through the property, and possibly agricultural buildings in the open area (Halifax Historical Society 1874). The tenant cabins on this map could have been former slave cabins.

In 1875, L. O. Gesner and William Cannon began buying portions of the surrounding fields and subdividing them for what became the town of Port Orange (Bathe 1955:120).

Daugherty continued to try to sell the balance of the plantation into the 1880s (Cardwell 2006:35–36). An 1882 account described it: "the famous Dunn Lawton plantation of a thousand acres, with extensive improvements of canals, ditches, clearings, buildings, all or part of which may be bought cheap with perfect title. This plantation is capable of yielding an ample support for a hundred families" (qtd. in Hawks 1977:31).

After William Daugherty's death, his son Charles inherited the property. At Charles's death, the plantation passed to his niece, Mrs. Austin Smith, who sold it to H. B. Simmons (Fitzgerald 1939:113). By 1890, the property was abandoned and one of the steam boilers was removed to a New Smyrna boatyard to steam ship timbers. Some of the gears were also removed to Daniel Lawton's shipyard in Daytona Beach (Bathe 1955:120).

Twentieth-Century Dunlawton. The last recorded use of the sugar works was in 1907, when residents of Daytona Beach reportedly took the bodies of nine stranded whales to the mill to render the whale oil using the old kettles and furnaces (Bathe 1955:121).

By the 1940s, Dunlawton was the property of J. Saxton Lloyd. Lloyd and Dr. Perry Sperber landscaped the property and attempted to develop a theme park known as Bongoland in honor of a baboon kept at the site. The life-size concrete dinosaurs now located in the gardens date from the Bongoland period and were reportedly donated by Dr. Sperber (Gardner 1977:40). After the theme park failed, Lloyd donated the property to Volusia County in 1963. In 1988, the county leased the park to the Botanical Gardens of Volusia, Inc., the present management (Burns 1988:9).

Dunlawton Sugar Works

This description of the Dunlawton sugar works is based on the 1991 and 2001 studies (Wayne et al. 1991; Wayne et al. 2001). The sugar works consisted of a single large structure, which was divided into an engine house, an open passageway with cane crusher, a boiling house, another passageway or work area, and the purgery (Figures 69 and 70). As late as the 1890s, the building retained its gable roof with a louvered, pyramidal roofed vent over the boiling room (Figure 71). Portions of the Cruger-DePeyster machinery installed by Marshall remain today.

Dunlawton is the only one of the sugar works to have a double sugar train.

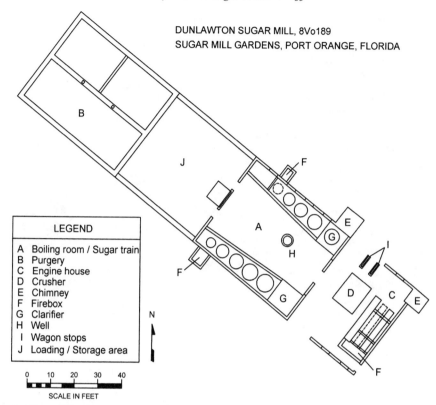

DUNLAWTON SUGAR MILL, 8Vo189
SUGAR MILL GARDENS, PORT ORANGE, FLORIDA

LEGEND

A Boiling room / Sugar train
B Purgery
C Engine house
D Crusher
E Chimney
F Firebox
G Clarifier
H Well
I Wagon stops
J Loading / Storage area

N

0 10 20 30 40
SCALE IN FEET

69. Plan of Dunlawton sugar works.

The 2001 study speculated that the sugar works may have originally consisted of the four-kettle train on the north side—possibly built by Dean or Bunch—which was later modified, probably by the Andersons, with the addition of the five-kettle train on the south (Wayne et al. 2001:173). The large purgery west of the boiling house (Figure 69) is comparable in size to those at Bulow and Cruger-DePeyster.

The walls of the Dunlawton ruins (Figure 72) are a combination of cut coquina blocks and bog rock (a hard limestone). The bog rock is denser and stronger than the coquina, which can result in stresses on the softer rock. Mortar is generously smeared in the joints between the stone. Both chimneys and lower portions of the north wall are built of cut coquina with well-done mortar joints. This suggests that the earlier Bunch/Anderson sugar works was built of cut coquina like those at the other plantations of the pre–Seminole War period, while the postwar rebuild by Marshall used bog rock on the coquina foundations of the destroyed mill. The exterior of the building was stuccoed, with scoring to give the appearance of regularly shaped stones (Piatek 1998:15).

Archaeological excavations completed at the northwest corner of the boiling

70. Looking northeast at Dunlawton sugar works.

71. Dunlawton sugar works in 1875. (Courtesy of the Halifax Historical Museum, Daytona Beach, Florida)

house and the north side of the boiling house chimney revealed that no builders trench was used for the boiling house; rather, the foundation rested directly on a natural clay deposit. The chimney, however, had a builders trench that yielded burned material—probably dating to the Seminole War destruction of the sugar works (Piatek 1998:10–11).

72. Northeast exterior wall at Dunlawton sugar works.

Engine House. The engine house has walls on the three exterior sides (north, south, and east) (Figure 69). Archaeologist Marilyn Stewart (1979:10) has pointed out that the existing structure is larger than the mill described in the Anderson claims; the Anderson sugar works would have extended only to the edge of the crusher and not to the south train. The west side of the engine house opens to the passageway between the engine house and boiling room (Figure 69). There is no indication that the walls continued between the engine house and boiling house; presumably this 15-foot-wide area was left open to provide access to and from the crusher for delivery of cane via the cane carrier described by the anonymous visitor (see Figure 9), and for removal of bagasse by wagons. The somewhat longer south wall of the engine room has two window openings while the north wall has a single window. Most of the east wall is missing, but late-nineteenth-century photographs show four windows in a 1½-story configuration (Figure 71). Deep pockets are located above the window sills on the jambs of the windows. These pockets were chipped out of the stone to hold boards for shutter hardware. The building walls have a coquina capstone but no visible footings or foundations.

There were originally two horizontal boilers in the engine room, supported by brick walls (Figure 69). Stewart (1979:10) identified the bricks as English—specifically Aston Wales—dating between 1841 to 1867, indicating that the supports date to the post–Seminole War period. The firebox is located at the south end of the boilers, where the remains of iron door frames are built into the brickwork (Figure 73). The boiler is made of cast-iron sections riveted together with cast-iron

73. Engine and boiler at Dunlawton sugar works.

end caps riveted to the end sections by internal integral flanges (Shepard 1977:1). Bathe (1955:117) says that this form of boiler construction was both cheap to manufacture and highly resistant to steam pressure. But the small diameter limited the amount of water the boilers could hold, thus requiring constant attention during operation. The boilers were connected by two cast-iron pipes at the top and bottom to maintain equal water levels and collect the steam. Bathe (1955:117) also says that the boilers would originally have been completely enclosed by masonry. Archaeological excavations in 1979 revealed a deep pit under the boilers, which might have served for air circulation to help prevent overheating of the boilers (Stewart 1979:8).

At the north end of the boiler, there is a brick flue leading to the chimney, topped with a steel grating (Figure 74). The primary firebox is at the south end of the boilers.

The west and south faces of the chimney have plaster lines marking the roof-line. The south side of the chimney has traces of plaster rusticated (a rough-hewn surface projecting from the joint lines, which are recessed and emphasized) to appear to be stone. The chimney is freestanding rather than interlaced with the adjacent walls and is flush with the north wall of the engine house. At the base of the north face of the chimney, there is a brick structure, which presumably functioned as a firebox to start a fire in the chimney to draw the heat through the flue from the boilers (Figure 75).

74. Engine house flue at Dunlawton sugar works.

Sugar Mill. Two brick-lined wagon stops are located in the passageway on the north side of the crusher, probably for bagasse removal (Figures 69 and 76). A ramp on the south side provided access for the cane carts or cane carrier coming into the crusher (Stewart 1979:10).

The remaining portions of the engine rest on a rebuilt coquina wall between the boilers and crusher. The engine remains consist of a horizontal cylinder with a pipe that connects it to a cubicle cast-iron box located 10 feet north above the cylinder (Figure 73). Cast Doric columns support the control piping connecting the box and cylinder. What appears to be part of a globe valve sits on top of the cylinder. A cast-iron throw and crankshaft are located to the east adjacent to the large flywheel. An offset circular cam wheel is mounted at the east side of the fly-wheel on the horizontal crankshaft. The six-foot-diameter flywheel consists of six cast-iron sections joined together by dovetailed flared metal tongues (Figure 73). A depression approximately two feet wide between the engine mount and crusher accommodated the flywheel (Shepard 1977:1–2). The crusher originally sat on a coquina-block base. Bearing journals on either side of the crusher were bolted to the masonry. The crusher consists of a main cogwheel on a cast-iron shaft, a set of cog gears, and three smooth cast-iron rollers approximately 21 inches in diameter and 42 inches long (Figure 77). The remains of a syrup pan rest beneath the rollers; the pan discharged via a spout on the north side (Shepard 1977:2). Bathe (1955:119) dated the mill to around 1830 based on its design.

Boiling House. The area between the engine room and the boiling house (Fig-

75. Firebox engine house chimney at Dunlawton sugar works.

76. Wagon stops at cane crusher at Dunlawton sugar works.

77. Cane crusher at Dunlawton sugar works.

ure 69) appears to have a paved floor. The east wall of the boiling room, like the south wall, is constructed of a mix of cut coquina block and bog rock, with coquina around the edges of the openings. Shepard (1977:3) identified five coquina jambs representing four or five openings in this wall. The east wall is comparable in thickness to the south wall. There is a cold joint between the north coquina-block train and the balance of the east wall, again perhaps as a result of the Marshall reconstruction of the sugar works. Bathe (1955:115) stated that the boiling house had a coquina rock floor.

The boiling house chimney (Figure 69) at the northeast corner of this part of the building extends to a ledge like that in the smaller engine house chimney. Both chimneys have a series of small openings at this ledge, which may have been for scaffolding. Like the engine house chimney, mortar marks the slope of the gable roof on the east face of the chimney. A brick arched flue opening is located at the west side of the chimney with an adjacent similar opening under the clarifier. Like the chimney of the engine house, this chimney is freestanding and separated by cold joints from the boiling house.

The north sugar train has a square fire chamber at the west end (Figure 69). The north wall of the chamber has a filled-in stone and brick arch—possibly an earlier flue. The south wall of the sugar train is bog rock over brick in the lower levels, while the east and west walls are brick. There are flue openings in both the west and north walls. The flues have a brick arch, and there is a rectangular opening with a flat iron lintel above the west flue; a second square opening is located above this lintel. The east wall adjacent to the end of the train has another brick arch, which has been bricked in—probably another flue. Archaeologist Ted Payne (personal communication 2001) and the author believe that this chamber was the original firebox for the north train when it was converted to a Jamaica train, and was later closed when the exterior firebox was added on the north side of the wall, matching the firebox of the south train (Figure 69).

Adjacent to the chimney, the north train has a large platform, which held the clarifier to receive juice from the crusher (Figures 69 and 78). The platform is brick, faced with coquina and shaped to fit the clarifier by being slightly domed in the center. A slot between the platform and the *grande* contains a cast-iron damper, which closed off the train from the chimney flue. This may have facilitated the operation of a single train at a time by focusing the heat on the south train, rather than on both trains. The remains of a riveted plate-iron clarifier sit on the platform. Shepard (1977:5) noted a sluice gate or spout on the west side of the clarifier remains with part of a control handle or lever, which fed the juice into the *grande* kettle. Contrary to the description of the Anderson sugar works, there were only four kettles in the train in the usual configuration of *grande* at the chimney end and *battèrie* or *teche* at the west end adjacent to the firebox. The kettles rested on brick supports, while the train was faced with coquina. The coquina had a ledge to support the workers' platform on the south side. Shepard (1977:5) recorded that an intact portion of the flue between the kettles showed the vaulted shape of the original flue. The brick-lined firebox under the western kettle has a metal flue and a portion of the grating that separated the fire from the ash level. The exterior firebox on the north side of the wall is below grade and rectangular in shape like that on the south side of the sugar works. The flue opening in the exterior firebox at the west end of the sugar train has the remains of iron hinges for the door. This brick-lined firebox steps down approximately two steps to the flue.

The well in the center of the boiling house (Figure 78) is built of bog rock. During the 1998 study, the well was cleaned and inspected. It was determined that a large pit was excavated to the water table. A large clear-glazed red earthenware liner was placed in the pit to line the well shaft. This liner rested on a timber and coquina foundation. A copper flange was placed on top of the liner, and another liner appears to have been placed on the first one, although the second liner is now missing. The top liner was later replaced by bog-rock stones built up above the surface. The top of the bog-rock liner has also been replaced, resulting in a slightly larger liner (Piatek 1998:16).

The south train was a five-kettle assemblage, with a coquina exterior and brick interior. There is a brick platform for the clarifier at the east end (Figures 69 and 79). This platform has two cast-iron dampers and a flue leading beneath the floor

78. Looking north at boiling house of Dunlawton sugar works.

to the chimney on the north side of the building (Figure 79). Shepard (1977:4) speculated that bricks visible in the floor of the east end of the boiling room are the arch of the subsurface flue. A horizontal damper on the west side of the platform allowed heat to rise under the clarifier, while a vertical damper adjacent to the flue stopped the heat from entering the flue. An opening in the south wall formed a firebox for supplemental heating of the clarifier. Part of a riveted plate-iron clarifier remains on the platform.

The north face of the south sugar train has a ledge approximately 10 inches below the existing brick lip to support the workers' platform. A piece of iron strap metal protrudes from the east end of this platform, perhaps to support the platform. The south train, like the north train, is brick faced with coquina. The brickwork around the kettles is beveled in a double sailor course to the level of the kettle rims. (A "sailor" refers to laying bricks with the long axis vertical and the wide side face out; a "soldier" is a vertical brick with the narrow side face out.) A notch in the brickwork between the *grande* and the *flambeau* may have supported a wooden framework above the five kettles.

In order to interpret the train, today the masonry supports for the kettles are shown in a sequence of stages of completion with the kettle at the firebox removed so that the firebox can be examined; the *grande* kettle area is fully constructed. A series of brick arched access ports are located on the south wall under each of the kettles (Figure 70). Due to the distance to the chimney, it is possible that this train

79. South train flue controls at Dunlawton sugar works.

required supplemental fires to maintain the heat. The primary firebox is located at the west end of the train on the south exterior of the building (Figures 69 and 80). This firebox is three feet deep with three crude steps leading down. The flue has an iron liner like that at the Oswald/Yonge Three Chimneys site. Similar iron liners may have been present in other flues at this site.

Two doors in the west wall provide access to the area between the boiling house and the purgery (Figure 69). Shepard (1977:4) estimated that the top of the wall corresponded to the wall height at the chimney in the northeast corner. There is no evidence of interior plaster in the boiling house.

The north wall of the boiling house has four evenly spaced windows. Like those in the engine house, these windows would have had wooden jambs. Presumably the south wall, which is missing above the level of the kettles, had a similar set of evenly spaced windows. One corner of the north exterior wall has traces of plaster scored to look like block.

Cooling Room. Coquina foundation walls span the space on the north and south sides between the boiling house and the purgery, forming a square room (Figure 69). The walls are exposed on the north side, but are subsurface on the south where their presence was documented by archaeological testing (Wayne et al. 1991:53). Presumably, the space between these two areas functioned much like that at Bulow for transfer of sugar to the purgery, and perhaps storage. The roof ventilator visible in Figure 71 was located over this area.

80. South train firebox at Dunlawton sugar works.

Purgery. The purgery is the same width as the rest of the building (Figure 69). The foundation walls are coquina blocks (Figure 81). Two wythes (single thickness) of brick line the interior of the purgery. The floor of the purgery is also lined with brick laid flat and coated with mortar or stucco. The brick floor slopes from west to east and is separated by an east-west partition constructed of cut coquina and bog rock, faced by brick. Two square holes evenly spaced in the center of this wall probably held vertical posts. A second north-south wall divides the north chamber in half; this wall is stuccoed brick. Based on a brick strip centered in the south chamber, a similar wall divided that space.

According to Bathe (1955:115), the purgery portion of the sugar works "was of wooden clapboard." This description is consistent with the remaining foundations, which have no evidence of missing upper masonry walls.

The Building. The historic photographs (Figure 71) show a continuous wood-shingled gable roof with a ventilator at the centerline of the building. The louvered ventilator is square with a pyramidal wood-shingled roof, possibly protected by metal caps over the hipped ridges. The east gable of the building roof is enclosed with horizontal wood siding, with two window openings in the attic level. The building also appears to have balloon framing in the purgery, a system in which the vertical studs extend in a single piece from the foundation sill to the roof plate (Putnam and Carlson 1974:35). Balloon framing was introduced to Florida after the Civil War, indicating that the building in the photographs is a postwar struc-

81. Looking northwest at purgery of Dunlawton sugar works.

ture (Herschel E. Shepard Jr., architect, personal communication 2008), although it probably closely resembles the original antebellum building due to the use of the coquina foundations and standing walls.

Based on an analysis of the older photographs, the overall building measurements, and the holes for columns in the purgery, Shepard (Wayne et al. 1991:68) speculated that the building was based on 10 equal bays with central support columns at the junctions of the bays. A smaller central bay corresponded with the ventilator location. The columns would have supported purlins that held the rafters, which rested on a ridge beam (see Wayne et al. 1991:70). Assuming that the entire complex from engine room to purgery was under a single roof, the resulting building would be approximately 181 feet by 43 feet in size (Wayne et al. 1991:60). This supports an 1870 description by Matthias Day that estimated that "the sugar house is probably 160 by 50 feet" (qtd. in Bathe 1955:113). It also matches well with the extant photographs of the Dunlawton sugar works (Figure 71).

In one of the historic photographs of the building, a large column is visible located against the north face of the cane crusher masonry supports. This would be at the quarter point of the span. A similar column was probably located on the opposite side of the crusher. The column placement supports the theory of a 10-bay building with a short bay in the center supporting the ventilator.

Dunlawton Summary. Not only does Dunlawton show the format of the complex, fully evolved sugar works, it also hints at the earlier simple form. Based on the bricked-in flues and the four-kettle configuration of the north train, this sugar works may have begun as a simple Spanish train during the Bunch period. Like McHardy, this four-kettle train was subsequently modified into a Jamaica train with a single flue. Then a second Jamaica train was added on the south side of the building by the Andersons, requiring a sophisticated underground flue system to connect it to the single chimney and regulate the heat flow in the two trains. Given the complex flues at Dunlawton, both the engineer and the sugar maker would have been very skilled.

Based on its design of a single large rectangular structure, with a sequence of work areas, Dunlawton may actually have had the most efficient layout of any of the East Florida sugar works, since cane would enter at one end and sugar would exit at the opposite end.

Summary of Fully Evolved Sugar Works

At the four fully evolved sugar works, we see operations constructed by people who were not only familiar with the sugar works of the Caribbean, and perhaps southeastern Georgia, but who anticipated producing sugar on a large scale. All used steam power, either in a separate building or in a separate zone of the sugar works. All presumably used horizontal crushers powered by the steam engines, probably fed by cane carriers. All had Jamaica trains. In the case of Dunlawton's double trains, a complex flue system was required to control the heat. These four sugar works are also large in size, again suggesting that their owners expected a high rate of production.

Finally, all four sugar works show a level of sophistication in their architecture and construction. They were built not only to be functional but also to reflect the investment the owners had made and the profits they anticipated. Features such as the careful symmetry of the structures, windows, and doors, and the stucco scored to appear to be stone, show an interest in creating buildings that looked good in addition to functioning. As architect Walt Marder said: "Of all the coquina resources, the sugar mills that remain are particularly symbolic of this once thriving plantation system which faded away. These huge factories, their plastered coquina walls embracing this major industry, today stand as mute evidence of that former time. And even today, they are still graceful, their stonework a wonderful testimony to the skill of their builders. Beautifully cut stone, fine, thin mortar joints, clean, precise lines, all bear witness to the once thriving society and the masterful workmen who populated the region" (Marder 2000:15).

9

The End of an Industry

[T]hese once thriving plantations, which were the culmination of many
years of hardship, tragedy and courage, . . . became ashes on the wind.
—Alice Strickland, *Ashes on the Wind: The Story of the Lost Plantations* (1985)

The eight sugar works discussed in this study were certainly not the only ones
that existed in East Florida. There were other large complexes like that of Major
Hernandez at St. Joseph's south of St. Augustine. And there were undoubtedly
numerous very small operations with one or two kettles, which basically produced
cane syrup and crude sugar for consumption on the farm or plantation. Unfortunately, little visible evidence remains of most of the sugar works in the region. In
other cases, what does remain is not readily accessible. The works examined in this
study are both the most accessible and, due to their condition, the most conducive
to analysis.

Comparison of Sugar Works

Figure 82 provides a single-page comparison of the eight sites. The most obvious
facts are the increase in size and complexity through time. Less than 100 years
separates the simple Spanish train of Oswald/Yonge Three Chimneys from the
complex double Jamaica trains of Dunlawton. But that was a critical time period in which sugar production went from an essentially hand-operated system to
a mechanized system. The problem to be solved in East Florida was how to make
sugar profitable. The architecture reflects the solution to that problem: adapting
to new technologies. The crucial adaptations were the Jamaica train with its single
flue and chimney; the horizontal crusher with a higher capacity and production;
and the steam engine, which provided greater, more reliable power along with
around-the-clock capability. These adaptations, in turn, led to changes in the
buildings themselves. Sugar works went from simple, probably open shelters, to
large masonry edifices. With the adaptation of more complex and expensive crushers and engines, there was a shift to enclosing the machinery in the buildings rather
than simply sheltering it under a post-supported roof.

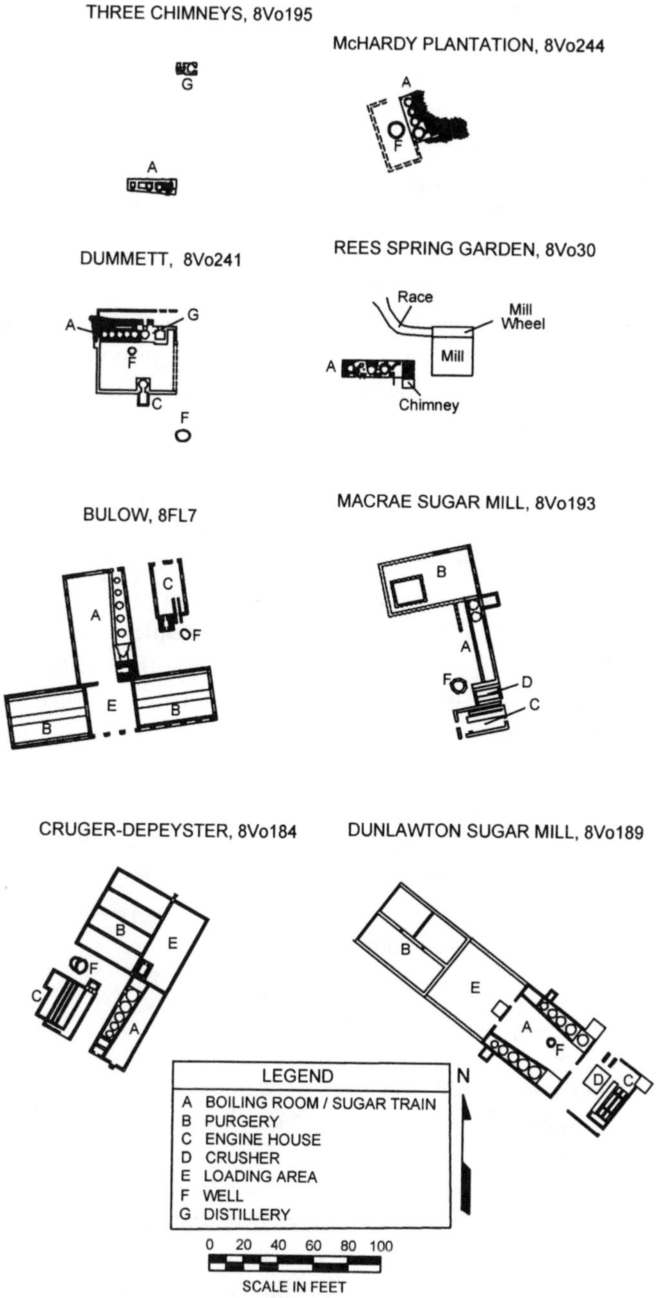

THREE CHIMNEYS, 8Vo195
G
A
McHARDY PLANTATION, 8Vo244
A
F
DUMMETT, 8Vo241
A
G
F
C
F
REES SPRING GARDEN, 8Vo30
Race
Mill
Wheel
Mill
A
Chimney
BULOW, 8FL7
A
C
F
E
B
B
MACRAE SUGAR MILL, 8Vo193
B
A
F
D
C
CRUGER-DEPEYSTER, 8Vo184
B
E
F
C
A
DUNLAWTON SUGAR MILL, 8Vo189
B
E
A
F
D
C
LEGEND
A BOILING ROOM / SUGAR TRAIN
B PURGERY
C ENGINE HOUSE
D CRUSHER
E LOADING AREA
F WELL
G DISTILLERY
N
0 20 40 60 80 100
SCALE IN FEET

82. Comparison of East Florida sugar works plans.

Each planter or engineer arranged the production system somewhat differently, although all of the operations required the basic crusher—possibly with an engine, a boiling house, and a purgery. We have examples of the engine and crusher located in separate areas such as Oswald/Yonge Three Chimneys, McHardy, Rees Spring Garden, Bulow, and Cruger-DePeyster, as well as consolidation of all activities into a single structure such as Macrae and Dunlawton. There are rectangular buildings such as McHardy, Dummett, and Dunlawton, as well as L shapes (Rees, Macrae, Cruger-DePeyster) and a T shape (Bulow).

The quality of construction is variable in the sugar works. Three Chimneys used what were essentially clinker bricks, but the masons were skilled in adapting the twisted shapes of these bricks to the round contours of the flues and kettles. Dummett displays a certain degree of experimentation with the native coquina stone in its use of a bracing battered wall and embedded arches to strengthen the masonry. Bulow and Macrae both display highly skilled and well-constructed masonry. But Cruger-DePeyster—notwithstanding its graceful arched windows and doors—has evidence of a less-skilled hand with its poor stone alignment and need for iron reinforcements. Dunlawton has a combination of well-built coquina walls and walls of bog rock, which required far less effort and skill.

The final point I have attempted to make in discussing the architecture of these eight sugar works is that, with the increased scale, complexity, and financial investment, there was also a greater effort to demonstrate the wealth (or potential wealth) and sophistication of the builders in the buildings themselves. Some features, such as the arched windows and doors of Bulow and Cruger-DePeyster, and the use of plaster or stucco over the coquina, facilitate the construction and stability of the buildings. At the same time, the symmetry and graceful design of the building openings and the rustication of the stucco to resemble stone suggest a desire to announce to the observer that this is the building of a successful, sophisticated owner. The same could be said of the recurring pattern of hiding less-finished masonry behind the equipment or under stucco.

Influences

The other theme that runs strongly through all of these sites is the connection to the Caribbean sugar industry, particularly that of the British Caribbean islands, and to sugar plantations in coastal Georgia. These buildings were not created in a vacuum. Many, if not most, of the owners were familiar with sugar making in the Caribbean and Georgia, while several owners imported engineers and sugar makers from the islands. Of course, the Georgia planters were also influenced by Caribbean sugar works. Planter James Hamilton Couper stated that his Hopeton sugar works in Georgia was "formed from a comparison of detailed drawings of sugar works in Louisiana, Jamaica and Demarara [Guyana]" (qtd. in Floyd 1937:95).

As architectural historian John Michael Vlach (1993:11) says: "Any plantation reflected not only the local ecology and climate, but the consequences of a particular settlement history as well." In both British Period Florida and the later Second Spanish and Territorial periods, the majority of the sugar planters had ties of some sort to the Caribbean, either through family or through previous experience. Folklorist Henry Glassie pointed out that the South in general is "more the northernmost point of the Caribbean than the southern extension of the Mid-Atlantic and New England" (qtd. in Joseph 1997:45–46). This would be particularly true of Florida, the closest of the southern states to the Caribbean, and the most similar in environment. As a result of the planters' personal connections to the Caribbean, as well as the similarity in environment and crop, the sugar works themselves strongly resemble their Caribbean predecessors. Clearly these planters recognized the wealth that the Caribbean sugar plantations yielded, and felt that they could duplicate these results in East Florida.

An Experiment Ends

Why did the sugar industry essentially end in East Florida after 1836? The easy answer is war—specifically the destruction of the sugar works by the Seminole in December 1835 and January 1836. As a local newspaper reported in 1836: "The whole of the country, south of St. Augustine, has been laid waste during the past week, and not a building of any value left standing. There is not a single house now remaining, between this city and Cape Florida, a distance of 250 miles, *all, all, have been burnt to the ground*" (*Niles Weekly Register* 1836b; emphasis in original). Historian Christopher Monaco (2005:152) points out that "Following the first wave of conflict, an entire industry lay in ruins—some two dozen sugar estates were destroyed south of St. Augustine alone."

The sugar works that were operating at that time were massive stone structures representing a significant financial investment. With the exception of Dunlawton and Spring Garden, why did the owners or other planters not attempt to reconstruct the buildings and reestablish the industry? The answer to that question is more complex and requires a broader view of the sugar industry.

First, the individual costs of reconstructing the masonry buildings and replacing damaged equipment, particularly steam engines, were significant. While the U.S. Congress did pay reparations for some of the damages of the Second Seminole War, these claims took years to settle, and often the settlement was less than the claims—or, as in the case of Bulow, was refused. Some of the planters, like Cruger and DePeyster, were already in debt before the sugar works were destroyed.

Finding the financing to reconstruct such expensive operations was undoubtedly difficult, if not impossible, in the years immediately following the war. It was probably far less expensive and faster to switch to another crop, or in some cases (such as Bulow) to simply abandon the plantations and let them return to nature. In addition to the costs of replacing the structures, the planters may have had to acquire additional slaves to replace those captured by or escaped to the Seminole during the war.

Second, and perhaps even more important, Florida could not compete with the sugar industry of the Caribbean, Brazil, and Louisiana, as well as the growing beet sugar production of Europe and the Midwest. By the time the steam-powered sugar works of Florida were first being built, "Louisiana was producing over 33,000 tons of sugar annually" (American Chemical Society 2007:1) from more than 300 plantations (Vlach 1991:38).

Third, on top of the competition, the price of sugar steadily dropped through the early years of the nineteenth century, to the point "that sugar was not the alluring crop that it appeared to be before the year 1831" (Floyd 1937:163). The result would be a property that required substantial financial investment but yielded a comparatively small quantity of product with a low value. Archaeologist Norman Barka (2001:141) points out that after the price of sugar collapsed in the 1840s, "sugar was no longer a luxury that could offset expensive transportation and the productive inefficiency of small plantations on marginal land." Not only were Florida's plantations generally smaller than those in Louisiana and Cuba, they were subject to occasional frosts and had less-fertile soils—all factors that made them marginal in the world market.

Fourth, when the Second Seminole War ended, sugar production in Florida shifted largely to Marion County and the southwest Gulf Coast (Cresap 1982:169). This shift may have been facilitated by the Armed Occupation Act of 1842, which provided land grants to those willing to settle in Central and South Florida. Historian Julia Floyd Smith (1973:11) has also explained that "sugar in Florida was in no way comparable to cotton as a money crop, and after 1850 its importance declined."

Fifth, Florida had fallen behind in terms of technological advances. Even the sugar works of Southwest and Central Florida that developed after the Second Seminole War continued to use the Jamaica train. But by the early 1840s, Louisiana's and Cuba's sugar producers had adapted the vacuum system of sugar production. John Heitman, a historian of the sugar industry, called this "the premier engineering achievement in nineteenth-century sugar technology," while others compared it to the cotton gin in terms of revolutionizing an industry (American Chemical Society 2007:1). This system produced better-quality sugar, used less fuel, was less wasteful, and required fewer workers. In fact, it is estimated that the combination of steam-powered crushers, vacuum pans, and centrifuges produced twice the sugar of older methods (Smith 2005:217). The bottom line was more profit for the sugar makers.

The end result was that, with the exception of Dunlawton and Spring Garden, the sugar works of East Florida were not reestablished after the Second Seminole War, and sugar ceased to be an important product in the region. We were left with "massive walls and finished arches, all of hewn stone, standing forth in strange and solitary grandeur amidst a wilderness of pine. . . . The bare walls are all that remain of this large establishment and these are fast falling into rubbish" (Strickland 1985:41).

References Cited

Adams, William Hampton
   1987   Plantation Archaeology: An Overview. In *Historical Archaeology of Planta-
           tions at Kings Bay, Camden County, Georgia*, pp. 9–22. *Reports of Investiga-
           tions* 5, Department of Anthropology, University of Florida, Gainesville.
Addison, John
   1819   Deposition, Report 1, Number 4 in *American State Papers* 5:376.
American Chemical Society
   2007   Sugar Production and the Multiple Effect Evaporator. Electronic document,
           National Historic Chemical Landmarks, http://acswebcontent.acs.org/
           landmarks/landmarks/sugar/sug3.html, accessed January 21, 2008.
Anderson, John, and Joseph D. Price
   ca. 1890 *The Walks, Drives and Sails of Ormond.* Lakeside Press, Portland, Maine.
Audubon, Lucy
   1879   *The Life of John James Audubon, the Naturalist.* E. P. Putnam's Sons, New
           York.
Baker, Henry A.
   1999   Fifteen Years on Bulow Creek: Glimpses of Bulowville. *Florida Anthropolo-
           gist* 52(1–2):115–123.
Barclay, Ceylon
   1994   *Red Rum Punch.* Cross Cultural Publications, Notre Dame, Indiana.
   1998   Three Chimneys . . . The Beginning. *Ormond Beach Historical Trust, Inc.
           Newsletter* 1(2):1, 5.
Barka, Norman F.
   2001   Time Lines: Changing Settlement Patterns on St. Eustatius. In *Island Lives:
           Historical Archaeologies of the Caribbean,* edited by Paul Farnsworth, pp. 103–
           141. University of Alabama Press, Tuscaloosa.
Barlow, James
   1826   Deposition of James Barlow for Reuben Loring v. Thomas H. Dummett.
           Box 134, Folder 11, St. Augustine Historical Society, St. Augustine, Florida.

Bathe, Greville
1955   *An Engineer's Note Book.* Press of Allen, Lane and Scott, Philadelphia.
Bishop, H. Radford
1975   Plantations along the Halifax. *Halifax Historical Herald* 4(2):1–14.
Boyd, Mark F.
1951   Florida Aflame: Background and Onset of the Seminole War, 1835. *Florida Historical Quarterly* 30: 1–115.
Burns, John R.
1988   The Story of Sugar Mill Gardens. *Leaflet* 4(4):7–9.
Burt, F. N.
1929   De Leon Springs, Florida. Self-published pamphlet. DeLand, Florida.
Butts, Eileen H.
1967   Richard Oswald (Born 1705–Died 1784). *Volusia County Record* 2(1):2.
Cardwell, Harold D., Sr.
1976   Return to Carrickfergus. *Halifax Historical Quarterly* 4(3):19–22.
1997   Bulow Plantation. In *Sites and Stories of Volusia County,* pp. 7–8. Volusia Anthropological Society, Ormond Beach, Florida.
2006   *The Story of Dunlawton Plantation.* Harold D. Cardwell Sr. and the Port Orange Historical Trust, Inc., Port Orange, Florida.
Carter, Clarence Edwin (editor)
1962   *The Territorial Papers of the United States.* Vol. 23, *The Territory of Florida, 1824–1828.* Government Printing Office, Washington, DC.
Carter, Thomas, and Elizabeth Collins Cromley
2005   *Invitation to Vernacular Architecture: A Guide to the Study of Ordinary Buildings and Landscapes.* University of Tennessee Press, Knoxville.
Chen, Ellen, and John F. Gerber
1990   Climate. In *Ecosystems of Florida,* edited by Ronald L. Myers and John J. Ewel, pp. 11–12. University of Central Florida Press, Orlando.
Cleland, John C.
1836   *The Superior Advantages to Be Derived from the Culture of Sugar-Cane, in East-Florida.* S. S. Miller, Charleston.
Coe, Capt. Chas. H.
1941   *Debunking the So-Called Spanish Mission near New Smyrna Beach, Volusia County, Florida.* Self-published, Washington, DC.
Cohen, Myer M.
1964   *Notices of Florida and the Campaigns.* Facsimile of 1836 edition. University of Florida Press, Gainesville.
Coker, William S., and Susan R. Parker
1996   The Second Spanish Period in the Two Floridas. In *The New History of Florida,* edited by Michael Gannon, pp. 150–166. University Press of Florida, Gainesville.
Cresap, Ida Keeling
1982   The History of Florida Agriculture: The Early Era. Manuscript on file,

The Hume Library, Florida Agricultural Experiment Station, University of Florida, Gainesville.

Cusick, James Gregory

2000   Spanish East Florida in the Atlantic Economy of the Late Eighteenth Century. In *Colonial Plantations and Economy in Florida,* edited by Jane G. Landers, pp. 168–188. University Press of Florida, Gainesville.

Daniel, Randy, Frank Sicius, and David Ferro

1980   *An Archaeological and Historical Survey of the Proposed Halifax Plantation Development, Volusia and Flagler Counties, Florida.* Bureau of Historic Sites and Properties *Miscellaneous Project Report Series* 52, Florida Division of Archives, History and Records Management, Tallahassee.

Davidson, Liliane

ca. 1950   Mysterious Old Ruins Found in Tomoka Region. Newspaper article on file, Halifax Historical Society, Daytona Beach, Florida.

1950a   1828 Court Controversy Shows 'Anacape' Ruins on Tomoka Were T. H. Dummett Sugar Mill. *Daytona Beach Evening News* March 26.

1950b   New Smyrna Ruins Mission Myth Corrected. *Daytona News Journal* April 30:23.

Denson, Robin L., Gary D. Ellis, and Russell Dorsey

1995   *Archaeological Survey of De Leon Springs State Recreation Area.* Ellis Archaeology/Gulf Archaeology Research Institute, Crystal River, Florida.

Dickison, Mary Elizabeth

1962   *Dickison and His Men: Reminiscences of the War in Florida.* Facsimile of 1890 edition. University of Florida Press, Gainesville.

Douglas, Lt. Col. John

1786   Affidavit Concerning Richard Oswald's Swamp Settlement. In *Loyalists in East Florida, 1774 to 1785; the Most Important Documents Pertaining Thereto, Edited with an Accompanying Narrative.* Vol. 2, edited by William Henry Siebert, 1972, pp. 59–61. Gregg Press, Boston.

Dummett, Anna Maria

1949   Remembrances of the Old Plantation. *Literary Florida,* February 1949.

Dunbar, J.

1980   *Archaeological and Historical Resource Assessment of Ponce De Leon Springs.* Florida Division of Historical Resources Master Site Files, Tallahassee.

Eubanks, Thomas Hales

1985   *Intensive Archaeological Testing at the John Houstoun McIntosh Sugarhouse, Camden County, Georgia.* Georgia Department of Natural Resources, Parks and Historic Sites Division, Historic Preservation Section, Atlanta.

1992   *Sugar, Slavery and Emancipation: The Industrial Archaeology of the West Indian Island of Tobago.* Ph.D. dissertation, University of Florida, Gainesville.

2004   Description of Thomas Spalding water mill. Posting to HISTARCH@asu.edu mailing list, October 19, 2004. Louisiana State Archaeologist, Baton Rouge, Louisiana.

Fabel, Robin F. A.
1996   British Rule in the Floridas. In *The New History of Florida*, edited by
        Michael Gannon, pp. 134–149. University Press of Florida, Gainesville.
Faust, Drew Gilpin
1991   Slavery in the American Experience. In *Before Freedom Came: African-
        American Life in the Antebellum South,* edited by Edward D. C. Campbell Jr.
        and Kym S. Rice, pp. 1–19. Museum of the Confederacy, Richmond, and
        University Press of Virginia, Charlottesville.
Fenty, Hazelle
1976   Camp Fagen. Newspaper article on file, Halifax Historical Society, Daytona
        Beach, Florida.
Fitzgerald, T. E.
1939   *Historical Highlights of Volusia County.* Observer Press, Daytona Beach,
        Florida.
Florida Department of Environmental Protection (FDEP)
1998   *Bulow Plantation Ruins State Historic Site Unit Management Plan.* Division
        of Recreation and Parks, Tallahassee, Florida.
Floyd, Marmaduke
1937   Part One. Certain Tabby Ruins on the Georgia Coast. In *Georgia's Disputed
        Ruins,* edited by E. Merton Coulter, pp. 1–189. University of North Carolina
        Press, Chapel Hill.
Forbes, William
1770   Letter to Andrew Turnbull. In Smyrnea: Dr. Andrew Turnbull and the
        Mediterranean Settlement at New Smyrna and Edgewater, Florida, 1766–
        1777, *Florida History Online,* http://www.unf.edu/floridahistoryonline/, by
        Daniel Schafer, p. 109, accessed August 8, 2009.
Ford, James A.
1937   Part Two: An Archaeological Report on the Elizafield Ruins. In *Georgia's
        Disputed Ruins,* edited by E. Merton Coulter, pp. 191–225. University of
        North Carolina Press, Chapel Hill.
Francke, Arthur E., Jr., Alyce Hockaday Gillingham, and Maxine Carey Turner
1986   *Volusia: The West Side.* West Volusia Historical Society, DeLand, Florida.
Galloway, J. H.
1985   Tradition and Innovation in the American Sugar Industry, c. 1500–1800.
        Annals of the Association of American Geographers 75(3):334–351.
1989   *The Sugar Cane Industry: An Historical Geography from Its Origins to 1914.*
        Cambridge University Press, Cambridge, England.
Gannon, Michael
1965   *The Cross in the Sand: The Early Catholic Church in Florida, 1513–1870.* Univer-
        sity of Florida Press, Gainesville.
2003   *Florida: A Short History.* University Press of Florida, Gainesville.
Gardner, Cherie
1977   Ruins of the Old Sugar Mill at Port Orange. *Halifax Historical Herald*
        5(2–3):38–41.

Genovese, Eugene D.
1962   The Significance of the Plantation for Southern Economic Development. *Journal of Southern History* 28:422–437.

Gluckman, Stephen J., and Henry A. Baker
1967   Archaeological Investigations at Bulow Plantation Ruins State Park: A Preliminary Report. Manuscript on file, Florida Master Site File, Tallahassee, Florida.

Gordon, Elsbeth K.
2002   *Florida's Colonial Architectural Heritage.* University Press of Florida, Gainesville.

Griffin, John W.
1951   Eyewitness Accounts Tell How Tomoka Blockhouse Was Hastily Built in 1836 to Fight Indians. *Daytona Beach Sunday News-Journal* April 8:19.
1952a   Dummett Sugar Mill, drawings. Florida Park Service Archaeological Survey. In the files of Patricia Griffin, St. Augustine, Florida.
1952b   Bulow House Ruins. Unpublished drawings, St. Augustine Historical Society, St. Augustine, Florida.
1952c   The Addison Blockhouse. *Florida Historical Quarterly* 30(3):276–293.
1993   Speech delivered to the Southeast Volusia Historical Society, January 16.

Griffin, Patricia C.
1999   The Halifax-Mosquitoes Plantation Corridor: An Overview. *Florida Anthropologist* 52(1–2):5–23.
2002   *Plantation Historical Research Conducted at DeLeon Springs State Park and the Immediate Surrounding Area Concerning the First Spanish Period until the 1870s When the Plantation Era Ended.* DeLeon Springs State Park, DeLeon Springs, Florida.
2003   Life on the Plantations of East Florida: 1763–1848. *Florida Anthropologist* 56(3):163–182.

Halcrow, Elizabeth M.
1982   *Canes and Chains: A Study of Sugar and Slavery.* Heinemann Educational Publishers, Oxford, England.

Halifax Historical Society
1874   Map of Dunlawton Plantation. Collections of the Halifax Historical Society, Daytona Beach, Florida.
1957   Article from *East Florida Herald*, February 8, 1825, copied by Ianthe Bond Hebel.

Hawks, Dr. J. M.
1977   Port Orange, Volusia County, Florida: A Tale of Two Cities. *Halifax Historical Herald* 5(2–3):31.

Hebel, Ianthe Bond
1955   "Strong Man of the Halifax" Could Tote Two 200 Pound Sacks of Potatoes. *Daytona Beach Sunday News-Journal* December 18:9A.

Hinkley, Ada Green
1931   *The Colonization of Ormond, Florida.* E. O. Painter, DeLand, Florida.

Historic American Building Survey (HABS)

1934   Mission of Atocuimi de Jororo. Measured drawings, data sheets, and photo-
        graphs. FL0303, HABS No. FL-15-4. Library of Congress, Washington, DC.

Historic Property Associates, Inc. (HPA)

1988   *Historic Properties Survey, New Smyrna Beach.* St. Augustine, Florida.

Humphries, George

1831   Deposition of George Humphries for Reuben Loring v. Thomas H. Dum-
        mett. Box 134, Folder 11, St. Augustine Historical Society, St. Augustine,
        Florida.

Hunter, Robert

1934   John Addison. *Daytona Beach News Journal* January 29.

Joseph, J. W.

1997   Building to Grow: Agrarian Adaptations to South Carolina's Historical
        Landscapes. In *Carolina's Historical Landscapes: Archaeological Perspec-
        tives,* edited by Linda F. Stine, Martha Zierdan, Lesly M. Drucker, and
        Christopher Judge, pp. 45–59. University of Tennessee Press, Knoxville.

Kipp, Gordon

1967   An Argument about History. *Daytona Beach Sunday News-Journal* Decem-
        ber 3:2E.

Lewisohn, Florence

1964   *Divers Information on the Romantic History of St. Croix.* St. Croix Landmarks
        Society, Frederiksted.

Loftfield, Thomas

2001   Creolization in Seventeenth-Century Barbados: Two Case Studies. In *Island
        Lives: Historical Archaeologies of the Caribbean,* edited by Paul Farnsworth,
        pp. 207–233. University of Alabama Press, Tuscaloosa.

Long, Edward

1774   *The History of Jamaica; or, General Survey of the Antient and Modern State of
        That Island.* 3 vols. Reprinted 1970, Frank Cass, London.

Loring, Reuben

ca. 1825 Bill to Col. Thomas Dummett. Box 134, Folder 11, St. Augustine Historical
        Society, St. Augustine, Florida.

1826   Bill to Col. Thomas Dummett. Box 134, Folder 11, St. Augustine Historical
        Society, St. Augustine, Florida.

1828   Deposition of Reuben Loring for Reuben Loring v. Thomas H. Dummett.
        Box 134, Folder 11, St. Augustine Historical Society, St. Augustine, Florida.

Mahon, John K.

1985   *History of the Second Seminole War, 1835–1842.* University Presses of Florida,
        Gainesville.

Marder, Walter

2000   Florida's Coquina Heritage. In *The Conservation and Preservation of Co-
        quina: A Symposium on Historic Building in the Coastal Southeast,* pp. 14–16.
        Division of Historical Resources, Florida Department of State, Tallahassee.

Martin, Sidney Walter

1944   *Florida during the Territorial Days.* University of Georgia Press, Athens.

McKee, Harley J.

1973   *Introduction to Early American Masonry, Stone, Brick, Mortar, and Plaster.* National Trust for Historic Preservation and Columbia University, New York.

McMurchie, John

1836   An Estimate of Machinery Connected to the Sugar Works Destroyed by the Seminole Indians on the Plantation of Dunnlawton Property of Messrs. George and James Anderson in January 1836. Deposition, State of South Carolina, Charleston District.

Meide, Chuck

2003   The Sugar Factory in the Colonial West Indies: An Archaeological and Historical Comparative Analysis. Manuscript provided by the author, St. Augustine, Florida.

Meniketti, Marco

2006   Sugar Mills, Technology, and Environmental Change: A Case Study of Colonial Agro-Industrial Development in the Caribbean. *Industrial Archeology* 32(1):53–80.

Mercer, Eric

1975   *English Vernacular Houses: A Study of Traditional Farmhouses and Cottages.* Her Majesty's Stationery Office, London.

Milanich, Jerald T.

1995   *Florida Indians and the Invasion from Europe.* University Press of Florida, Gainesville.

Mintz, Sidney W.

1985   *Sweetness and Power: The Place of Sugar in Modern History.* Viking Penguin, New York.

Monaco, C. S.

2005   *Moses Levy of Florida: Jewish Utopian and Antebellum Reformer.* Louisiana State University Press, Baton Rouge.

Motte, Jacob Rhett

1953   *Journey into Wilderness: An Army Surgeon's Account of Life in Camp and Field during the Creek and Seminole Wars, 1836–1838.* Floridiana Facsimile and Reprint Series, University of Florida Press, Gainesville.

Moultrie, Lieutenant Governor John

1786   Deposition Concerning Mount Oswald Plantation. In *Loyalists in East Florida, 1774 to 1785; the Most Important Documents Pertaining Thereto, Edited with an Accompanying Narrative.* Vol. 2, edited by William Henry Siebert, 1972, pp. 57–59. Gregg Press, Boston.

Mowat, Charles Loch

1964   *East Florida as a British Province, 1763–1784.* Floridiana Facsimile and Reprint Series, University of Florida Press, Gainesville.

Mullenix, Matt
2007   Sugar at LSU: A Chronology. Electronic document, www.lib.lsu.edu/
        special/exhibits/sugar/contents.html, accessed January 22, 2008.
Myers, Ronald L., and John J. Ewel
1990   *Ecosystems of Florida.* University of Central Florida Press, Orlando.
Niles Weekly Register [Baltimore, Maryland]
1836a   The Seminole War. February 27, 13(26):441.
1836b   The Seminole War. February 6, 13(26):393–394.
Olcott, Henry S.
1857   *Sorgho and Imphee, The Chinese and African Sugar Canes: A Treatise upon Their
        Origin, Varieties, and Culture....* A. O. Moore, Agricultural Book Publishers,
        New York.
Orser, Charles E., Jr.
1984   The Past Ten Years of Plantation Archaeology in the Southeastern United
        States. *Southeastern Archaeology* 3(1):1–12.
Parks, John, and Kathryn Younkin
2004   *Historic Structure Report, The Historic Addison Blockhouse, 8Vo193.* Renker
        Eich Parks Architects, Inc., and Architecture and Historic Preservation,
        St. Petersburg, Florida.
Payne, Robert
1786   Deposition regarding Mount Oswald Plantation. In *Loyalists in East Florida,
        1774 to 1785; the Most Important Documents Pertaining Thereto, Edited with
        an Accompanying Narrative,* Vol. 2, edited by William Henry Siebert, 1972,
        pp. 56–57. Gregg Press, Boston.
Payne, Ted M.
1995   *Archaeological Assessment for the Three Chimneys Site and a Reconnaissance Sur-
        vey at a Project Land Parcel, Ormond Beach, Florida.* MAAR Associates, Inc.,
        Newark, New Jersey.
1996a   Richard Oswald's British Period Sugar and Rum Production: Three Chim-
        neys Site (8Vo196). Paper presented at Annual Meeting, Florida Anthropo-
        logical Society, Sarasota, Florida.
1996b   *Limited Archaeological Investigations at 8Vo244 to Establish a Construc-
        tion Date for Structure 1; Bulow Creek State Park, Volusia County, Florida.*
        American Preservation Consultants, Inc., St. Augustine Beach, Florida.
1999   Preliminary Archaeological Investigations at the Moultrie/Bunch/Dummett
        British through Territorial-period Plantations. *Florida Anthropologist*
        52(1–2):103–114.
2002   *Archaeological Investigations at the Nineteenth Century Sugar Boiling Facility
        and the Immediate Area in DeLeon Springs State Park, DeLeon Springs, Florida.*
        DeLeon Springs State Park, DeLeon Springs, Florida.
2007   *Archaeological Excavation of Soil from the Eastern-most Firebox in the Sugar
        Boiling Feature, Three Chimneys Site (8Vo196), Ormond Beach, Florida.*
        American Preservation Consultants, Inc., St. Augustine Beach, Florida.

Payne, Ted M., and Patricia C. Griffin

2001   *Sugar Making in East Florida and the History of Eight Plantations.* American Preservation Consultants, Inc., St. Augustine Beach, Florida.

Peterson, Curtiss E.

1978   Report on Dunlawton Sugar Mill, Volusia County. Manuscript on file, Volusia County, DeLand, Florida.

Piatek, Bruce John

1998   *DunLawton Sugar Factory: Archaeological Study and Stabilization.* Ormond Beach, Florida.

2000   *Archaeological Testing of the Boiler Room Walls, New Smyrna Sugar Mill Ruins (8Vo184—The Cruger and DePeyster Mill).* Bruce Piatek and Associates, Ormond Beach, Florida.

Porter, Charlotte M.

2009   Artists-Naturalists in Florida. Electronic document, Florida Naturalists, Florida Museum of Natural History, Gainesville, www.flmnh.ufl.edu/naturalists/audubon01.htm, accessed August 4, 2009.

Proby, Kathryn Hall

2002   *Audubon in Florida.* University of Miami Press, Coral Gables, Florida.

Proctor, Samuel

1975   Introduction. In *Eighteenth-Century Florida and Its Borderlands,* edited by Samuel Proctor, pp. v–xii. University Presses of Florida, Gainesville.

Prunty, Merle, Jr.

1955   The Renaissance of the Southern Plantation. *Geographic Review* 65(4):459–491.

Putnam, R. E., and G. E. Carlson

1974   *Architectural and Building Trades Dictionary.* 3rd ed. American Technical Society, Chicago.

Reeves, I. S. K., V

ca. 1979 Dunlawton. Manuscript on file, Architects Design Group, Inc., Winter Park, Florida.

Rivers, Larry Eugene

2000   *Slavery in Florida: Territorial Days to Emancipation.* University Press of Florida, Gainesville.

Ross, Malcolm

1773   Letter to Richard Oswald, Esq., Philip Lane, London, July 11, 1773. Manuscript on file, Ted M. Payne, St. Augustine, Florida.

Roughley, Thomas

1823   *The Jamaica Planter's Guide; or, a System for Planting and Managing a Sugar Estate, or Other Plantations in That Island, and throughout the British West Indies in General.* Longman, Hurst, Rees, Orme, and Brown, London, England. Manuscript on file, St. Augustine Historical Society, St. Augustine, Florida.

St. Johns County Court Records

1846   William Kemble v. William DePeyster, 131–139. St. Augustine, Florida.

Satchell, Veront

1997   The Diffusion of the Watt Steam Engine in the Jamaican Slave/Sugar Economy, (1810–1830). Paper presented at XXIX Conference Annuelle de L'Association des Historiens de la Caraibe, Martinique.

2002   Steam for Sugar-Cane Milling: The Diffusion of the Boulton and Watt Stationary Steam Engine to the Jamaican Sugar Industry, 1809–1830. In *Jamaica in Slavery and Freedom: History, Heritage and Culture*, edited by Kathleen E. A. Monteith and Glen Richards, pp. 242–258. University of the West Indies Press, Barbados.

Schafer, Daniel L.

1982   "settling a colony over a bottle of claret": Early Plantation Development in British East Florida. *El Escribano* 19:37–53.

1999   Mount Oswald Plantation at Tomoka and Halifax Rivers. *Florida Anthropologist* 52(1–2):25–30.

2000   "A Swamp of an Investment"? Richard Oswald's British East Florida Plantation Experiment. In *Colonial Plantations and Economy in Florida*, edited by Jane G. Landers, pp. 11–38. University Press of Florida, Gainesville.

2008   Smyrnea: Dr. Andrew Turnbull and the Mediterranean Settlement at New Smyrna and Edgewater, Florida, 1766–1777. Electronic document, *Florida History Online*, http://www.unf.edu/floridahistoryonline/, accessed August 8, 2009.

Schene, Michael G.

1976   *Hopes, Dreams, and Promises: A History of Volusia County, Florida.* News-Journal Corporation, Daytona Beach, Florida.

Schery, Robert W.

1952   *Plants for Man.* Prentice-Hall, Englewood Cliffs, New Jersey.

Shepard, Herschel E., Jr.

1977   *The Dunlawton Sugar Mill, A Report.* Fisher and Shepard, Architects and Planners, Inc., Jacksonville, Florida.

Shepard, Herschel E., Jr., James Moore, Jason O'Brian, Glenn Spotts, Li Wang, Yingxian Zhang, and Lucy B. Wayne

2000   *Early Sugar Plantations in Florida: A Preliminary Inventory of Representative Sites.* ARC 6821 Graduate Seminar, School of Architecture, University of Florida, Gainesville.

Siebert, Wilbur Henry (editor)

1972   *Loyalists in East Florida, 1774 to 1785; the Most Important Documents Pertaining Thereto, Edited with an Accompanying Narrative*, Vol. 2, Records of their Claims for Losses of Property in the Province. Gregg Press, Boston.

Singleton, Theresa A.

1985   *The Archaeology of Slavery and Plantation Life.* Academic Press, Orlando, Florida.

Sitterson, J. Carlyle

1953   *Sugar Country: The Cane Sugar Industry in the South, 1753–1950.* University of Kentucky Press, Lexington.

Smith, Frederick H.

2005   *Caribbean Rum: A Social and Economic History.* University Press of Florida, Gainesville.

Smith, Greg C., Marsha A. Chance, and Keith H. Ashley

1994   *A Cultural Resource Assessment Survey of the New Smyrna Sugar Mill Ruins (8Vo184—The Cruger and Depeyster Mill), Volusia County, Florida.* Environmental Services, Inc., Jacksonville, Florida.

Smith, Julia Floyd

1973   *Slavery and Plantation Growth in Antebellum Florida, 1821–1860.* University of Florida Press, Gainesville.

Smith, W. W.

1836   *Sketch of the Seminole War and Sketches during a Campaign.* Dan J. Dowling, Charleston, South Carolina.

Southeast Volusia Chamber of Commerce

1997   Sugar Mill Ruins, New Smyrna Beach, FL. Flyer, Visitor Information Center, New Smyrna Beach, Florida.

Spalding, Thomas

1816   *Observations on the Method of Planting and Cultivating the Sugar-Cane in Georgia and South Carolina.* Agricultural Society of South Carolina, Charleston. Reprinted in *Georgia's Disputed Ruins,* E. Merton Coulter, pp. 227–263. University of North Carolina Press, Chapel Hill.

Stanton, Edith P.

1942   Addison Plantation One of the Most Prominent during the Second Spanish Occupation. *Daytona Beach Observer* October 8.

1949   *Ruins of the Early Plantations of the Halifax Area, Volusia County, Florida.* Volusia County Historical Society, Daytona Beach, Florida.

Stewart, Marilyn C.

1979   The Dunlawton Sugar Mill Archaeological Project. Manuscript on file, Volusia County, DeLand, Florida.

Strickland, Alice

1957   The Dummett Family Saga. *Journal of the Halifax Historical Society* 2(1):3–14.

1963   *The Valiant Pioneers: A History of Ormond Beach, Volusia County, Florida.* Center Printing Company, Miami, Florida.

1966   Personal notes taken from *Memoir of Admiral John Bunch Bonnemaison McHardy.* Manuscript on file, St. Augustine Historical Society, St. Augustine, Florida.

1976   Richard Oswald, Florida's Revolutionary War Hero. *Volusia County Record,* Bicentennial Issue, December 1976:3–4.

1985   *Ashes on the Wind: The Story of the Lost Plantations.* Volusia County Historical Commission, Daytona Beach, Florida.

Taylor, Thomas Walter

ca. 1980 The "Old Chimneys" of Ormond Beach. Manuscript on file, Halifax Historical Society, Daytona Beach, Florida.

1984   *"Settling a Colony over a Bottle of Claret": Richard Oswald and the British Settlement of Florida.* M.A. thesis, University of North Carolina, Greensboro.

Van Horn, James

1826   Deposition of James Van Horn in Reuben Loring v. Thomas H. Dummett. Box 134, Folder 11, St. Augustine Historical Society, St. Augustine, Florida.

Vaux, William Percival

1853   Sale of Dunlawton Plantation to James and S. P. Ravenel. Miscellaneous Record Book A, Volusia County Courthouse, DeLand, Florida.

Vignoles, Charles

1823   *Observations upon the Floridas.* Facsimile edition, 1977. University Presses of Florida, Gainesville.

Vlach, John Michael

1991   Plantation Landscapes of the Antebellum South. In *Before Freedom Came: African-American Life in the Antebellum South,* edited by Edward D. C. Campbell Jr. and Kym S. Rice, pp. 21–49. Museum of the Confederacy, Richmond, Virginia, and University Press of Virginia, Charlottesville, Virginia.

1993   *Back of the Big House: The Architecture of Plantation Slavery.* University of North Carolina Press, Chapel Hill.

Ward, J. R.

1988   *British West Indian Slavery, 1750–1834: The Process of Amelioration.* Clarendon Press, Oxford University Press, Oxford, England.

Warren, Evelyn V.

1989   *History of DeLeon Springs (Spring Garden).* Friends of DeLeon Springs, DeLeon Springs, Florida.

Wayne, Lucy B., Martin F. Dickinson, and Greg Hall

1999   *An Historic Preservation Plan for the Three Chimneys Sugar Mill Site (8Vo196), Ormond Beach, Florida.* SouthArc, Inc., Gainesville, Florida.

2001   *Sugar Plantation Heritage Tourism Plan, Task I: Structural Stabilization Study.* SouthArc, Inc., Gainesville, Florida.

Wayne, Lucy B., Martin F. Dickinson, and Herschel E. Shepard Jr.

1991   *Sugar Mill Botanical Gardens Archaeological and Architectural Study, Dunlawton Sugar Mill, 8Vo189, Volusia County, Florida.* SouthArc, Inc., Gainesville.

Wells, Camille

1995   New Light on Sunnyside: Architectural and Documentary Testaments of an Early Virginia House. *Bulletin of the Northumberland County Historical Society* 32:3.

Williams, John Lee

1837   *The Territory of Florida.* A. T. Goodrich, New York.

Wills, Eric

2009   Guarding the Glories of San Juan. *Preservation* 61(1):16–23.

Wilson, Emily F.

1957   The Plantation Area—Maps. *Journal of the Halifax Historical Society* 2(1):15–23.

Wilson, Ruth Danenhower
1945   The Bulow Plantation, 1821–1835. *Florida Historical Quarterly* 23(4):229–240.
Works Progress Administration (WPA)
1940   *Spanish Land Grants in Florida, Vol. 2, Confirmed Claims A-B-C.* Historical
         Records Survey, Division of Professional and Service Works Projects.
         Manuscript on file, St. Augustine Historical Society, St. Augustine, Florida.
1941   *Spanish Land Grants in Florida, Vol. 4, Confirmed Claims K–R.* Historical
         Records Survey, Division of Professional and Service Works Projects.
         Manuscript on file, St. Augustine Historical Society, St. Augustine, Florida.
Wray, Leonard
1848   *The Practical Sugar Planter: A Complete Account of the Cultivation and Manu-
         facture of Sugar Cane, according to the Latest and Most Improved Processes.*
         Smith, Elder and Company, London.
Zierdan, Martha
1986   The Rural-Urban Connection in the Lowcountry. *South Carolina Antiquities*
         18(1–2):33–40.

Index

Page numbers in italics refer to figures and tables.

Adams-Onis Treaty of 1819, 40
adaptation of power sources, 99–100
adaptive sugar works, 73–74, 97
Addison, John, 110–11
Addison, Thomas, 111
Addison Blockhouse, 111, 112
Addison plantation, 109
advancements in sugar boiling, 29
advantages of steam engines, 25
advertisement: of Dunlawton property, 134;
    McHardy's plantation, 67; for mill sup-
    plies, 23
aesthetics of buildings, 50
agro-industry, sugar plantations as, 12
Anacape. *See* San Antonio de Anacape
analysis of Dunlawton building, 145–46
Anderson, Sarah Perry, 131
Anderson ownership of Dunlawton, 131–33
animal powered mills, 22, *23, 24,* 73
annual rate of return, 40
Antigua, boiling house in, *30*
Antilles, sugar works in, *21*
archaeological and architectural investiga-
    tions, 53
archaeological findings: Addison-Macrae
    site, 109–10; Bulow, 100; Cruger-
    DePeyster site, 119, 123; Dummett site,
    75, 76, 80; Dunlawton site, 130, 135–36;
    McHardy site, 66; Oswald/Yonge Three
    Chimneys, 53, 63; Spring Garden site,
    88, 96

arches, wall, *84, 85, 86*
architectural, and archaeological investiga-
    tions, 53
architectural influences, 47, 49, 98, 150–51
architecture, variations of, 7
architecture, vernacular, 47
Atocuimi de Jororo, Mission of. *See*
    Cruger-DePeyster
attacks: at Bulow plantation, 102; at Dun-
    lawton plantation, 132; at Macrae plan-
    tation, 112
Audobon, John James, 91, 101, 103

bagasse, 23
bagasse house, 19, *22*
bailing from kettles, 28
balloon framing, 145
barrels, rum, 34
Bathe, Greville, 130
battèrie, 26
beginning of sugar making, 28
benefit-cost ratio, 39
Berry's Premium Firebricks, 69, *71*
Blockhouse, Addison, 111, 112
bog rock, 134
boiler area, Macrae, *115*
boiling cane juice, 25–26
boiling houses: Antigua, *30;* Bulow, 105,
    107, *107;* Cruger-DePeyster, 126–27, *127;*
    Dunlawton, 137–38, *138,* 139, 141, *143*
boiling sugar and sugar cones, *29*

Bongoland, 134
boundaries, East Florida, 5
bricks: Berry's Premium Firebricks, 69,
    71; Oswald/Yonge train, 59–60; Spring
    Garden, 96
British period, 36–38
building, Dunlawton sugar works, 145–46
building layouts, 49–50
building materials, 50–51
Bulow, Charles Wilhelm, 101
Bulow, John Joachim, 101–102
Bulow plantation: acquiring, 101; boiling
    house, 107, 107; engine house, 105–7, 105,
    106; plantation, 100–102; purgeries, 107–
    8; site information, 8; site of, 100; spring
    house, 109; sugar works, 102–4, 103
Bunch: Cecily, 131; John, 66, 67, 76, 131;
    Mary Dean, 66
Bunch-Dummett ownership, 76–77
Bushnell, John, 66

Camp M'Rae, 112
cane, varieties of, 16–17
cane carrier, 23, 24, 106, 139
cane crusher, Dunlawton, 139, 140, 141
cane harvest, 19, 20
cane mill, 106
cane reproduction, 17
Caribbean architectural influences, 49,
    150–51
Caribbean sites, 99
Carrickfergus and Second Seminole war, 112
Carrickfergus plantation, 109, 111
causes of failure of East Florida sugar in-
    dustry, 151–52
challenges for sugar plantations, 38–39
characteristics, similarities of geographic, 6
characteristics of plantation system, 10–11
"Chimney," the, 58
chimneys: Cruger-DePeyster, 128; Dum-
    mett site, 80–81, 80, 81, 87; Dunlawton,
    138, 140, 141; McHardy, 68, 70, 71; Spring
    Garden, 89, 96; steam power and, 25;
    Three Chimneys, 65
cisterns, 31, 32
claims, damage, 42–43, 55, 132
clarification process, 26
clarifier, 22, 25

claying process, 31–32
cleaning the sugar works, 19
Cleland, John, 39–40
climate, 6
clinkers, 59
coagulators, 28
Coe, Charles H., 119, 121
comparison of all eight sugar works sites, 8,
    148–50, 149
comparison of Caribbean and East Florida
    sites, 99
competition in sugar market, 42–44, 152
Connor, Jeanette Thurber, 120–21
Connor, Washington E., 120
Conrad-Oates Company, 68
construction: costs of, 78; of Cruger-
    DePeyster site, 127–28; of Dum-
    mett sugar works, 76–77; of trains, 28;
    of Macrae sugar works, 113; quality of
    Cruger-DePeyster site, 122; records at
    Dummett site, 77
contact information, site. See visitor infor-
    mation
coolers, 29
cooling area, Macrae, 117–18
cooling process, 29, 30, 31
cooling room, 144
coquina, 51
Corbin, 56
cost-benefit ratio, 39
costs: of construction, 78; estimation of,
    39–40; to planters, 42; of rollers, 22; of
    sugar, 39; of sugar works, 99
Creek Indians, 36
crop maintenance, 17
Cruger-DePeyster plantation: boiling
    room, 126–27, 127; engine house, 123–24,
    125; engine house and well, 126; engines,
    122–23; history of, 119–20; purgery, 129;
    site information, 8; sugar works, 118–19,
    122–23, 123
crusher, cane, 139, 140, 141
crusher area, Macrae, 115
curing house, 32
curing process, 31
Currick Fergus, 111
cush-cush, 33
cutting sugar cane, 19, 20

Daugherty ownership, 133–34
Dean, Patrick, 131
defecator, *22, 25*
DeLeon Springs legends, 89
DeLeon Springs State Park, 88. *See also*
    Spring Garden
De Leon, Ponce, 89
designer, building, 103
distillery: Dummett, *82,* 86; Oswald/Yonge,
    63, *64;* rum, 33–34, *34;* Three Chim-
    neys, *65*
dogtrot house, 90
double sugar train, 134–35
draining room, 31. *See also* purgeries
Douglas, Lt. Col. John, 55
Dummett: Anna, 76, 78–79; Thomas, 76, 111
Dummett-Bunch ownership, 76–77
Dummett plantation: history of, 75–76;
    purgery, 78–79; site information, *8*
Dummett sugar works: construction rec-
    ords, 77; elevation of, 80, *84;* interior and
    exterior, 80, *83, 84;* looking northeast at,
    80; looking southwest at, *81;* plans, *82,*
    149; power sources, 74; remains, 79, 82–
    83, 85; train, 81
dunder, 33
Dunlawton plantation: engine house, *139;*
    firebox, *145;* history of, 130–34; map,
    133–34; restoration of sugar works, 130;
    site information, *8;* south train flue con-
    trols, *144;* sugar trains, 141–44
Dunlawton sugar works: boiling house, *143;*
    the building, 145–46; chimney, *140;* de-
    scription of, 134–36; engine and boiler
    at, *138;* location of, 129–30; northeast,
    136; northeast exterior wall of, *137;* plans,
    135, 149; purgery, *146*

East Florida: boundaries, 5; sugar planta-
    tions, 5, *8,* 36, *149;* sugar works, *4*
economics of East Florida sugar produc-
    tion, 43–44
efficiency of animal powered system, 73
1819 Treaty of Adams-Onis, 40
1823 Treaty of Moultrie Creek, 41
elevation of Dummett sugar works, 80, *84*
Ellis Archaeology/Gulf Archaeology Re-
    search Institute, 88

end of Florida sugar production, 44
end of sugar industry, 3, 148, 151–52
end products of sugar making, 32
engineer, building, 103
engine house: Bulow, 105–7, *105, 106;*
    Cruger-DePeyster, 123–24, *125, 126;* flue
    at Dunlawton, *139;* Macrae, 113
engines: area at Macrae, *115;* Cruger-
    DePeyster, 122–23; at Dunlawton sugar
    works, *138;* steam, 74, *78,* 83, *85*
Environmental Services, Inc., 119
estimates, cost, 39–40
estimates, production, 13
evaporation system, multiple-effect, 29
experimentation: with growth and produc-
    tion, 38; with power sources, 74, 99–100;
    in sugar processing, 73
export, sugar as an, 35

Fagan, William, 56
Fagan House at Oswald/Yonge Tree Chim-
    neys, 57, *58,* 60
failure of plantations, 38–39
farm versus plantation, 10
fermentation, methods of, 33
financing plantations, 42, 120
firebox engine house chimney at Dunlaw-
    ton sugar works, *140*
fireboxes: at Dummett sugar works, *85, 86,*
    87; at Dunlawton sugar works, *145;* of
    Macrae sugar train, *116;* Oswald/Yonge
    Three Chimneys, 61; side-by-side, 63
First Spanish Period, 35–36
flambeau, 26
flaws, animal powered system, 73
flaws, steam engine, 74
Flegert, William H., 57
Florida militia, 102
Floyd, Marmaduke, 121
flue controls at Dunlawton, *144*
flues: at Dummett site, 86; under *grande*
    kettle, Oswald/Yonge, *62;* iron, 61;
    liner, 144
flywheel, sugar mill, 139
Forbes: James, 89; William, 76
framing, balloon, 145
Franciscan mission, 120–21
French train. *See* Jamaica trains

frontier institution, 11
fully evolved sugar works, 98, 147
furnace, 27–28

Garden Spring, 91
geography, similarities of site, 6
geography of East Florida, 5
Georgian architectural influences, 150–51
grande, 26
Grant, Governor James, 53
grants: land, 37; McHardy, 67; Mount Os-
    wald, 54; Spring Garden, 89; system, 90
granulation test, 28–29
Griffin, John W., 66, 75, 100, 109, 119
Griffin, Patricia, 38, 88
growing sugar, 16–17

Hall, Thomas H., 131
harvesting cane, 19, 20
Harwood, Norman, 68
Henry Yonge plantation, 52–53
history: Addison-Macrae holdings, 110–11;
    and architecture, 47; Bulow plantation,
    100–101; Cruger-DePeyster plantation,
    119–20; Dummett plantation, 75–76;
    Dunlawton site, 130–31; McHardy site,
    66; Oswald/Yonge Three Chimneys, 53;
    Spring Garden, 88–89; sugar, 14, 16
hogsheads, 31
horizontal mills, 22–23, 24
houses: Bulow main, 101; Bulow spring,
    108–9; curing, 32; at Dummett site, 76
Hull, Ambrose, 119

identified as Spanish mission, 79
impurities, 26
indigo, processing, 56
industries, plantations as, 12
industry, end of sugar, 3, 148, 151–52
influences, architecture, 47, 48
influences, Caribbean and Georgian,
    150–51
innovations in sugar processing, 23, 73
institution, frontier, 11
interior of Dummett sugar works, 80, 83, 85
invasion of Bulow plantation, 102
invasion of Macrae plantation, 112
inventory of Dunlawton, 133–34

investigations, archaeological and architec-
    tural. See archaeological findings
invoice, construction, 77–78

Jamaican sugar plantation, 13
Jamaica trains, 26, 27, 68, 73, 93
joints, 87
Jororo, mission, 120

Kemble, William, 120
kettles. See trains
King's Road, 6

labor, slave, 13
laborers, Seminole Indians as, 102
labor per acreage cultivated, 17
land grants. See grants
lawsuits: against Cruger-DePeyster, 120; at
    Dummett, 76, 78
Lawton, Joseph and Charles, 120, 131
layouts, building, 49
legends of Deleon Springs, 89
Levy, Moses Elias, 41–42
live-oaker, 133
Lloyd, J. Saxton, 134
loading/storage room, Bulow, 107–8, 108
loading/storage room, Cruger-DePeyster,
    127–28
locations of slave cabins, 99
locations of sugar works, 4, 8
Loring, Reuben, 76–78, 103
Louisiana sugar production, 29, 38–39, 43,
    129, 152
low wine, 34
L-shaped layout, 22, 22, 49

Macrae, Duncan, 103, 111
Macrae, Kenneth, 111
Macrae engine/boiler/crusher area, 115
Macrae plantation: site information, 8;
    sugar train, 115, 116; sugar works, 109–10,
    112, 113; sugar works plans, 114
maintenance, crop, 17
making rum, 33–34, 34
map of Dunlawton, 133–34
Marshall, John, 120, 133
masonry, Dummett site, 87–88
"McCreigh" plantation, 103

McHardy, John B. B., 67, 131
McHardy, Robert, 66–67, 110
McHardy plantation: land grant, 66;
    ownership, 66–68; plan of sugar works,
    70; purgery, 68; site information, 8; sugar
    train and well, 69; sugar works, 68–69;
    sugar works chimney, 71; walls, 68
McMurchie, John, 131–132
militia, Florida, 102
milling sugar cane, 19, 22
mills: advertisement of supplies for, 23;
    animal powered, 23, 24, 73; cane, 106;
    horizontal, 22–23, 24; steam powered,
    23, 25; vertical, 22, 23
mill wheel, 93, 94, 95
missions, 79, 120–22
Mitchell, John R., 131
molasses, 19, 32, 39
Moncrief, James, 66
Moncrief Damietta tract, 67
mortar, 60–61, 69, 87
Mosquito grant, 67
Mosquito Roarers, 102, 132
Moultrie, John, 54, 55, 75
Moultrie Creek, 1823 Treaty of, 41
Mount Oswald grant, 54
multiple-effect evaporation system, 29

names of kettles, 26
National Register of Historic Places, 7, 8,
    53, 102, 119, 130
native materials, 72
net proceeds, 40
New Britain, 57
New Smyrna colony, 37, 76, 119
New Smyrna Sugar Mill, 118–19
"noble cane", 16
Norris, Major George, 92
north train, Dunlawton, 141–42

Oglethorpe, General James, 89
"Old Chimneys", 58
operators, steam, 74
Ormond Beach, 37, 56
Ormond Beach Historical Society, 52, 57
Oswald, Richard, 37, 53, 54
Oswald ownership, 53–56
Oswald's Swamp Settlement, 52–53

Oswald/Yonge Three Chimneys: archaeo-
    logical findings, 53, 63; chimney, 65; dis-
    tillery, 64; flues, 62; history, 53–57; land
    grant, 54; site information, 8; sugar
    train, 58–59, 60–62; sugar works, 57, 149;
    visitor information, 52; well, 65
Otaheite, 16–17
overflow, 28
overseers, Oswald plantation, 54
ownership: Connor, 120–21; Cruger-
    DePeyster, 119–20; Daugherty, 133–34;
    Dummett, 77–79; Dunlawton, 131–33;
    McHardy, 66–68; Oswald, 53–57; Rees, 91;
    of sites, 8; Woodruff, 90–91; Yonge, 56

pancake restaurant, 88, 89
Panton, William, 89
park information. See visitor information
Patriot War, 40, 90
pattern, settlement, 11
Payne, Robert, 55
Payne, Ted, 38, 53, 66, 75–76, 88, 109–10
Period: British, 36–38; First Spanish, 35–
    36; Second Spanish, 38–41, 90; Territo-
    rial, 41–42
Peterson, Curtiss, 130
Piatek, Bruce, 130
plans: Bulow sugar works, 104, 149;
    Cruger-DePeyster sugar works, 122,
    124, 149; Dummett sugar works, 82,
    149; Dunlawton sugar works, 135, 149;
    East Florida sugar works, 149; idealized
    sugar works, 22; Macrae sugar works,
    114, 149; McHardy sugar works, 70, 149;
    Oswald/Yonge Three Chimneys site, 59,
    149; Rees Spring Garden sugar works,
    94, 149
plantations: challenges for, 38–39; defini-
    tion of, 10–11; description of, 3; lists of
    the eight, 8, 149; Rosetta, 75–76; success
    of individual, 37; versus farms, 10
plantation system, southern, 11
plantation system characteristics, 10
planters in East Florida, 37, 39
planting cane, 17
planting sugar cane in Antigua, West In-
    dies, 18
plaque, Bulowville, 103

plaster rusticated surface, 138
Poaceac, 16
Port Orange, 129, 134
postcard, Bulow Ville, 103
post-Dummett ownership, 79
post-McHardy ownership, 67–68
post-Seminole war, 92–93, 102
post-Seminole war ownership of Dunlawton, 133
post-sugar ownership, 56–57
power sources, 73, 74
preparing sugar works for production, 19
prices: molasses, 39, rum, 39; sugar, 39, 152
problems of financing Cruger-DePeyster, 120
problems of Florida sugar production, 44
process, beginning of sugar making, 28
processing, improvements in sugar, 29
processing sugar, 19
producers, large sugar, 43
producing rum, 33–34, 34
production, peak, 41
production, sugar, 3, 16
production estimates, 13
proof, rum, 34
propre, 26
publications, local history, 51
puncheons, 34
purgeries, 19, 22, 32, 49. See also individual
plantations
purging house, 31

questions, sugar works, 51

"ratoon cane", 17
raw sugar, processing, 19
reales, 39
recommendations, architecture, 49
Rees Spring Garden. See Spring Garden
Rees, Colonel Orlando, 88, 91–92
remains, distillery, 63–65
remains of East Florida sugar works, 153
reproduction, cane, 17
restaurant, pancake, 88, 89
restoration of Dunlawton sugar works,
130, 131
"ribbon cane", 16–17
rollers, 22–23, 24
Rollestown colony, 37

Rosetta plantation, 75–76
ruins of sugar house, 121
rum, 32–33
rum distillery, 33–34, 34
rumors of Deleon Springs, 89
rum prices, 39
Russell, James 100–101
rusticated surface, plaster, 138

saccharometer, 26
Saccharum, 14
Saccharum officinarum, 15, 16
"sailor", 143
sale of rum, 34
sales history of Dunlawton, 131, 134
salt production, 133
San Antonio de Anacape, 79
sawmills, Bulow, 105–6
Schafer, Daniel, 53
"scum" kettle, 28
Second Seminole War, 102
Second Seminole War, effects of, 41, 132
Second Seminole War and Carrickfergus, 112
Second Spanish Period, 38–41, 90
selling Swamp Settlement, 57
selling values of sugar, 39
Seminole Indians, 36, 79, 102
Seminole War, post, 102
separation of sugar and molasses, 31
settlement history, Oswald, 53–56
settlement pattern, 11
settlements, lack of, 6
seventeenth century sugar works, 21
Shepard, Herschel, 100, 110, 130
side-by-side fireboxes, 63
similarities of fully evolved sugar works, 147
similarities of sites geography, 6
sirop, 26, 59
site number and ownership, 8
site plans, 49
sites, Caribbean, 99
skimmers, 28, 29
skirmishes, Seminole War, 132
slaked lime, 28
slave cabins, 11, 99, 101
slave labor, 13
Smoak, E. B., 68, 79

soils, 6, 16–17
"soldier", 143
sources of power, 73
SouthArc, Inc., 53, 66, 75, 88, 100, 119, 130
Southern Agriculturist, 48
southern plantation system, 11
south train, Dunlawton, 142–43
south train firebox at Dunlawton, *145*
south train flue controls at Dunlawton, *144*
Spalding, Thomas, 22, 31, 49, 74
Spanish mission, misidentified as, 79
Spanish Period, First, 35–36
Spanish Period, Second, 38–41, 90
Spanish trains, 26, *27*, 68, *69*, 72
Sperber, Dr. Perry, 134
Spring Garden: history of, 88–89; modern
    waterwheel, *94;* ownership, 90–91; site
    information, *8;* sugar works, 89, 93, 96–
    97, *149;* waterwheel in late nineteenth
    century, *94*
Spring Garden at DeLeon Springs, power
    sources, 74
spring house, Bulow, 108–9, *109*
Starke, John, 92
Starke, Thomas, 92
Statehood, 42–44
steam engines, 74, *78,* 83, *85*
steam powered mills, 23, *24,* 25
still, rum, 33–34, *34*
storage/loading room, Bulow, 107–8, *108*
storage/loading room, Cruger-DePeyster,
    127–28
strike pans, 27, 28
structures, variations of, 7
stucco: Cruger-DePeyster, 127, 129; Dum-
    mett, 83, 88; Dunlawton, 145; scoring, 51;
    use of, 150
sugar: boiling, 25–26, 29; cane, 14, *15,* 16,
    39; cones, *29;* as an export, 35; growing,
    16–17, *18;* labor, 13, 17, 102; making, 28;
    milling, 19, 22; peak production of, 41;
    prices, 39; processing, 19; production, 3,
    13, 43; purgery, *32*
sugar boiling house in Antigua, *30*
Sugar Bowl of Louisiana, 43
sugar industry, end of, 3, 148, 151–52
Sugar Mill Botanical Gardens, 129
sugar trains. *See* trains

sugar works: in Antilles, *21;* description
    of, 19, *21;* fully evolved, 98, 147; ground
    plan, *22;* locations of, *4;* as missions, 121;
    plans, *59;* remains, 3; in Surinam, *75*
Sun Trust Investment Company, 57
Surinam, sugar works in, *75*
surveys, 66
Swamp Settlement, *8,* 37, 52–57
Swift Brothers, 56

tabby: concrete, 31; mortar, 60, 63; plaster,
    85, 88, 113, 117
teche, 26
technology, changes in, 50, 152–53
"tempering", 26
Territorial Period, 41–42
test, granulation, 28–29
theme park, Bongoland, 134
theory, mission, 121–22
Three Chimneys site, 52–53, 58. *See also*
    Oswald/Yonge Three Chimneys
Tomoka grant, 67
Tomoka State Park, 66, 68
Tour through the Island of Jamaica in the
    Year 1823, 74
tract, Moncrief Damietta, 67
train and well, McHardy, *69*
training steam operators, 74
trains: Bulow, 104, *104;* construction, 28;
    Cruger-DePeyster sugar, 126–27; de-
    scription of, 26; Dummett sugar, 81, 86–
    87; Dunlawton double sugar, 134–35,
    141–44; Jamaica, 26, *27,* 68, 73, 93; kettle,
    26, *27;* Macrae sugar, 115, *116;* McHardy
    sugar, 68, *69;* Oswald/Yonge Three
    Chimneys, 57, 58–59, *60–62;* Spanish,
    26, 27f, 72; Spring Garden, 93, *95,* 96
"trashing canes", 17
Treaty: of 1819, Adams-Onis, 40; of Moul-
    trie Creek, 41; of Paris, 55
T-shaped layout, 49
Turnbull, Andrew, 76, 119, 130
Turnbull settlement, 76, 89
twentieth-century Dunlawton, 134
types of kettles, 26

undershot wheel, 91, 93
Union soldiers at Spring Garden, 92

vacuum pans, 29
varieties of sugar cane, *15,* 16–17
vats, 25–26
Vaux, William P., 133
vernacular architecture, 47
vertical mills, 22, *23*
visitor access, Bulow sugar works, 104
visitor access, Cruger-DePeyster, 123
visitor information: Bulow, 100; Cruger-DePeyster, 118; Dummett, 75; Dunlawton, 129; Oswald/Yonge Three Chimneys, 52; Spring Garden, 88

wagon stops at Dunlawton sugar works, *140*
wall arch, Dummett, *86*
walls: Cruger-DePeyster, 125, 127–28; Dummett sugar works, 85; Macrae sugar works, 113–14
war, post-Seminole, 92–93, 102, 112
war and East Florida sugar industry, 151
wash combinations, 33

water-powered mill, 74
website. *See* visitor information
wells: Bulow, 106–7; Cruger-DePeyster, 124, *126;* Dummett, 83, 86; Dunlawton, 142; Macrae sugar works, *117;* McHardy sugar train and, *69;* Three Chimneys, *65*
West Indies: boiling house, *30;* harvesting in, *20;* planting sugar cane in, *18;* sugar works, *21*
wheel, mill, 93
Williams, William, 88, 90
windmill power, 74
wine, low, 34
Woodruff: Jane, 90–91; Joseph, 88, 90–91
worm pipe, 33–34, *34*

yield, sugar cane, 39
Yonge, Henry, 56
Yonge ownership, 56
Yonge Three Chimneys, Oswald. *See* Oswald/Yonge Three Chimneys